Junior Athletics
for
Playground and Field

Jim Hall

A & C Black • London

First published 2001 by
A & C Black (Publishers) Ltd
37 Soho Square, London W1D 3QZ

© Jim Hall 2001

ISBN 0 7136 5824 X

A CIP catalogue record for this book
is available from the British Library.

Cover illustration by Eleanor King

Note
Whilst every effort has been made to ensure that the content of this book is as
technically accurate as possible, neither the author nor the publishers can accept
responsibility for any injury or loss sustained as a result of the use of this material.

Printed and bound in Great Britain by
Bell & Bain Ltd, Glasgow

CONTENTS

INTRODUCTION

The Junior School athletic activities lesson aims to enable pupils to experience:

(a) vigorous, enthusiastic participation in running, jumping, throwing, hurdling and relays, which are all natural and enjoyable activities, worth doing for their own sake and as contributors to normal growth and development;
(b) varied and challenging activities and practices designed to improve, develop and refine techniques in running, jumping, throwing, hurdling and relays;
(c) a series of simple tests with measurements of 'How fast?', 'How far?' and 'How high?' to allow pupils to measure, compare and improve their own performances, and be aware of their progress and achievement from lesson to lesson;
(d) competition, which includes competing against their own previous best, against others, and, as a team member, against other teams;
(e) competitions that they and others have combined to plan and create, experience, reflect on and develop;
(f) the motivation – inspired by the excitement and pleasure of participation and progress – to continue practising to improve the skills of running, jumping and throwing, which also play a big part in most of our major team games.

The lesson plans and their accompanying notes are designed to help teachers and schools provide lessons that give variety, challenge, progression and, most importantly, almost non-stop action for all with the minimum of waiting, watching or queuing.

Individual scoring charts provide a unique record of progress which, almost without exception, will take place as the term goes on and pupils benefit from regular practice, encouragement and enthusiastic teaching.

Jim Hall
July 2001

FACILITIES FOR JUNIOR SCHOOL ATHLETIC ACTIVITIES

(1) An on-site playing field, marked for running, relays, throwing and jumping practices is the ideal. If the field is big enough for one winter games pitch, a 200 m, six-lane oval track can be fitted in. The straight of 75–100 m, with six lanes along the side of the field nearer to the school, will extend beyond both bends in the track. The long straight on one side, the shorter straight on the far side, the circular track and the markings for throws and jumps placed centrally within the track, provide an excellent group of facilities for interesting and varied lessons.

- Bigger fields allow a track of 250 or 300 m with useful longer straights on both sides and more space within for markings for throwing and jumping practices.
- If there is space, a long jump facility with its own run up and sand box needs to be sited parallel to one of the boundaries of the field, away from the lines of the winter games pitch.
- For most schools high jumping will be careful, low scissors jumping from grass to land on grass if there is no deep safety mat of nylon/PVC with an anti-slip rubber base.
- Ideally, the long straight will be on the side of the track nearer the school so that the newly arrived class can be warmed up quickly on or around that straight. The straight is also used for timed sprints over 50–75 m, relays and hurdling practices during the group activities.
- Within the track, four or five sets of lines

from which to throw tennis balls, large balls, hoops, quoits and bean bags are marked so that they do not interfere with one another. Additional lines are marked at appropriate distances from the throwing lines to accommodate most pupils' performances.

(2) Travelling to an off-site playing field still takes place if a school has no field, but the cost of travelling, hiring and marking has meant that many schools either can no longer travel off-site, or can only afford to send their oldest age group. Once again, a 200–300 m track, with a long straight on one side and markings for throwing and jumping activities will be needed.

(3) The school playground now has to be the athletic activities teaching space for the majority of junior school pupils. While it lacks the space and the potential of a reasonable sized field, the playground is usually adjacent to the school, which means a shorter distance to carry the equipment, and its permanent line markings make it a satisfactory, multi-activity teaching space for running, relays, hurdling, throwing and jumping.

Demonstrations of good work can be more easily given and more easily observed and commented on, when pupils are reasonably close together on the playground.

There will be days when a wet, muddy or unmarked field, or one with long, uncut grass will not be a suitable place to take pupils. The playground will be suitable almost every day.

EQUIPMENT FOR JUNIOR SCHOOL ATHLETIC ACTIVITIES

(1) Running, relays, hurdling

- Twelve 12 inch or 18 inch marker cones for marking starts and finishes, relays, and as supports for canes to make 'hurdles'. These marker cones will also be used in games lessons to make goals, mark out small-sided rounders areas, and act as wickets in small group cricket games.
- Fifteen relay batons can be of alloy or polypropylene, or made from sawn-up broom handles or the hard cardboard cylinders within rolls of dressmaking material.
- 1 stopwatch.
- A set of small cone-shape markers for starts, finishes and relays, if the marker cones are all being used as hurdles.

(2) Throws

- 1 x 50 m measuring tape
- 1 or more long, 24 inch skipping ropes, with coloured tape stuck on at 1 metre intervals to place alongside throwing areas. This serves as a quick measurement aid to the receiving, judging, marking partner.
- 12 plastic, dome-shape markers to be used to mark distances thrown by one's partner

Sets of fifteen :
- tennis balls
- large balls
- hoops
- quoits
- bean bags

(3) Jumps

- 1 set high jump stands
- 1 high jump bar
- 1 weighted rope
- Long piece of elastic to tie between the stands as an inexpensive substitute for a high jump bar. The elastic 'bar' is used in lessons because it does not hurt shins or impede the jumper if struck – it bounces safely out of the way.
- 15 garden canes measuring 1 metre for practising scissors and standing high jumps

with a partner. These canes also give hurdling practice when placed on the ground or on two marker cones. Ends of canes must be set into a cork from a wine bottle or wrapped with tape to prevent accidents if they are struck and fly up.

Metre sticks, placed on the ground, parallel to the jumps, are useful in precise measurements of standing long jumps and partner or team standing long jumps.

Carriage and storage

Inexpensive, zip-top, plastic, 18 inch x 12 inch x 24 inch holdalls with handles are recommended containers and storers for the equipment. Each should be spacious enough to hold 12 large balls.

TIMETABLING THE JUNIOR SCHOOL ATHLETIC ACTIVITIES LESSON

A typical weekly allocation of time for physical education in a junior school is the one hour games lesson, plus two half hours for gymnastic activities and dance. A recommended weekly athletic activities lesson during September, and from April until July, can be arranged by using one of the three traditional lesson times, because games, gymnastic activities and dance should be well provided for during the autumn and winter.

For the approximately twelve weeks from April to July, the four different summer term lessons, each running for three weeks, can be programmed in blocks of 3 x 30 minutes, using the dance or gymnastic activities times, alternating with blocks of 3 x 50 minutes in the games lesson times.

LESSON PLAN • 30–50 minutes athletic activities lesson

WARM-UP ACTIVITIES   3–4 minutes

Walking; jogging; running for style, quietness, straightness; good striding; 'feeling' a running rhythm; sprinting.
Running to practise and recall lap and playground circuit speeds and rhythms.

'Follow the leader', copying, and side by side, same speed.
Team jogging and sprinting from end to front of team.

TIMED LAP, LAPS OR PART LAP ON THE FIELD OR A TIMED CIRCUIT ON THE PLAYGROUND   3–5 minutes

100–300 metres, depending on age and previous experience on the track or circuits of netball courts on the playground.

CLASS ACTIVITY   5–8 minutes

Whole class work at the same skill, often with a partner. Suitable activities include:
(1) Throwing tennis ball, large ball, hoop or quoit.
(2) Putting bean bag as in shot put.

(3) Scissors jump and standing high jump over a low cane held by partner.
(4) Relay baton exchange with a partner.
(5) Scaled-down long and triple jumps.
(6) Hurdling over canes on the ground.

GROUP ACTIVITIES IN SIXES, the ideal number for pairing many of the practices   16–28 minutes

Five groups (in class of thirty) rotate around the varied throws, sprints, hurdles, relays and 'fun runs'.

(e) RELAYS   3–5 minutes

Occasionally with a partner. Mostly in teams of six: shuttles, lines, around track or playground circuit.

This opening part of the lesson prepares the class physically, putting them in the mood for their vigorous activity in the fresh air. We need to stimulate action in pupils who have probably come from being sedentary in the classroom.

Many of the warming up activities take place on the longer straight of the track which should be on the side nearer the school to allow a near-instant start within seconds of arriving on the field. On the playground, the class will gather behind one of the end lines of the netball courts for any end-to-end jogging or running, or they will be well spaced out within the court or courts for individual, partner or group practices.

As well as stimulating thoughtful, lively leg activity, we aim to establish a well-ordered and co-operative atmosphere without which a full and enjoyable lesson is impossible, particularly on the large teaching space of the field.

Because the warm-up is a whole-class activity, with everyone working at the same skill, it is a good opportunity to teach and coach good technique in the walking, jogging and running that are usually involved. We move to warm up for its own sake, but we also practise good quality movement in a thoughtful, focussed way. Pupils should complete these start-of-lesson practices feeling physically alive and ready, and showing an improved technique.

Examples of warming up and introductory activities

(1) Easy jogging with arms and heels low, alternating with faster running with arms, knees and heels all lifting higher.

(2) Jog forward, then sprint between two marked lines, counting the number of times you strike the ground with the foot that first hits the line. Now, repeat the activity, emphasising a full knee lift which can add inches to each stride. Count again and see if your good knee lift reduces the number of strides you need.

(3) Easy, non-stop jogging for 30 seconds. 'Coast along comfortably.'

(4) Teams of six jog behind a leader. End runner sprints up to front by leaning forward and stretching out the strides. 'Jog...jog...sprint...jog.'

(5) Pairs, cruising one behind the other, avoiding other couples, at an easy cruising speed. On 'Change!', the following partner sprints to take the lead, trying to repeat the same cruising speed.

(6) Jog easily at a speed you think you can maintain for a minute.

(7) Run, emphasising the strong drive of the rear leg for power. This is accompanied by a slight forward lean of the whole body.

(8) Follow your leader who will plan to show you three lively, athletic leg actions. Can you build up to working in unison?

(9) Run beside a partner, keeping together at the same, easy 'cruising'-speed rhythm. Are you quiet and lifting heels, arms and knees?

(10) Run and practise a hurdling action to see which foot you lead with. It rises straight up and down in the same line. The rear, trailing leg comes around and down to clear the imaginary hurdle. Aim for 'Over, pull round, 1, 2, 3; over, pull round, 1, 2, 3.'

(11) Quick walking, jogging, running, alternately.

This timed activity follows on from being warmed up and takes place early in the lesson while the pupils still feel lively and strong enough to do it well. The distance will usually be in the range of 100–300 m, depending on age, experience and air temperature.

Inexperienced, under-exercised and possibly unfit junior school pupils might think that a run of 150 m is a 'long distance' – it is designed to make them breathe deeply and perspire freely in a way that is seldom part of their inactive, mostly sedentary lifestyles experience.

It is hoped that junior school classes, having followed a challenging physical education programme with plenty of timed, short/middle distance runs in their athletic activities lessons, will be keen to test themselves, without any physical distress. It is also hoped they have reason to be proud of the many recorded and improved times over distances from 50–300 m, and pleased at their obvious improved level of fitness.

Organising timed laps or part laps on field and circuits on playground

(1) Class line up in groups of six, behind one another, at a starting position on the track or playground. Each group is given its order of moving off (e.g. Group 1 down to Group 5) and they are told the distance and where the run starts and finishes.

(2) Each group in turn starts off on a signal and starting time from the teacher. 'Group one, no seconds on the watch, go! Group two, five seconds, go! Group three, ten seconds, go!' (etc)

(3) All run round and finish, running past the teacher who is now positioned at the end of the field lap or playground circuit. Runners listen to their finishing times being called out by the teacher. Their own time is then worked out by subtracting starting time from finishing time.

(4) While the class recovers, the teacher checks on 'Any new personal best times? How many of you were steady and equalled or nearly equalled your previous best time? How many of you feel you have recovered quickly? Who felt that you spread your effort sensibly around the whole of the distance?'

(5) The teacher gives praise and expresses pleasure at the improvements that have come from trying hard, performing with determination, and planning sensibly how to run the distance.

(6) If the subtraction of first time from second time is a problem it can be eased by having groups start at 10 second intervals, remembering the two times and checking back in class with help.

(7) Back in class, times will be recorded on individual score cards. Dramatic improvements can be made during the athletic activities season, and it is not unknown for youngsters to start running for pleasure and improvement in their own time.

Class activities are used to teach one activity easily and thoroughly, developing the skill, step by step to the teacher's command. The planning, performing and reflecting, which are an essential feature of physical education in the National Curriculum, can also easily be included and encouraged here.

Where there is sufficient space and equipment the whole class works at the same skill. With the whole class doing the same activity all teaching has relevance for everyone. All safety points; all coaching of main features; all praise for good quality work; and all demonstrations will apply to everyone.

Sometimes, because of lack of space on a playground or, more commonly, because there is insufficient equipment, a second activity has to be taught at the same time.

Teaching only one activity means that the practising can be tightly controlled and developed by the teacher. If the skill of throwing a tennis ball, large ball or hoop, for example, is not closely supervised, it can degenerate into a wild throwing contest with more time spent chasing after wayward implements than practising good technique.

Examples of class activities skills practices

Running
(1) Relay baton exchange with a partner.
(2) Hurdling over line of canes on the ground or on pairs of cones.
(3) Sprinting to see how far you can run in 5 seconds. Partner marks distance reached as teacher calls 'Five!'
(4) Finding own easy, cruising rhythm, sustainable for one minute without distress.
(5) Running 10–15 m, counting number of strides between markers. Repeat exercise, with greater emphasis on good knee and heel lift and reach, to extend stride for greater speed.
(6) Running with 'straight ahead' action in legs, arms, head and shoulders, and finishing fast to take you past the end line.

Throwing
(1) Throwing a tennis ball.
(2) Throwing a large ball from above and behind the head, with straight arms, as in football throw in.
(3) Throwing a hoop or quoit, as in discus fashion.
(4) Putting a bean bag from against the neck, as in shot put.
(5) Aiming/throwing to land tennis ball or large ball in a target area.

Jumping
(1) Scissors jump over a low cane, held by partner, after a short run up.
(2) Standing high jump over a low cane, held by a partner.
(3) Standing long jump by self; with a partner; or as one of a team.
(4) Scaled down long jump after a short run up to take-off line.
(5) Scaled down hop, step and jump after a short run up to take-off line.
(6) Plan and practise own sequence of two or three different jumping actions from: one foot to other foot; one foot to both feet; one foot to same foot; two feet to two feet; two feet to one foot.

Group activities are the most important part of the lesson. A well-ordered class, working quietly, wholeheartedly, safely and sensibly at its five different athletic activities is one of the most pleasing sights within junior school physical education.

Because many of the group activities are done with a partner, a group of six is ideal. Six enables pupils to have three pairs for relay practices, or two threes for a shuttle relay. Six permits three to throw a ball, bean bag, quoit or hoop for a partner to mark, measure and send back for the next throw. Pairs can practise high jumping over a cane held low by a partner.

After the teacher says 'Go to your starting group places, please', he or she should check the numbers in each group. If two of the groups have five, the teacher should transfer one pupil to make a six and a four for pairings.

Running to the starting group place speeds up the change from class activities to group activities. Pupils have only one group to remember from lesson to lesson. From this starting position, the groups can be rotated round, clockwise and anti-clockwise, on alternate lessons, to ensure that they experience all five activities at least twice. In the 50-minute lesson programme, they should experience all the activities every lesson.

Good behaviour and sensible, co-operative practising are essential to the success of the varied group-work where groups are working by themselves for most of the time. If they cannot be trusted to behave properly, the teacher will have to persist with whole-class teaching until the class is trained to a satisfactory level in behaviour, attitude and sociability.

Formal teaching, with the class moving only on the teacher's command, and reducing the extent of the lesson plan are necessary when an element within the class is not:

- responding readily to instructions
- being physically active
- following relevant rules and safety procedures
- being mindful of others
- trying hard to succeed.

Group work provides variety and something that appeals to each pupil. It always includes running, jumping and throwing; gives further practice of the class activity just experienced; allows time for the repeated, focused practice, essential to learning and understanding; enables progress to be measured, recognised and recorded.

The order of rotating around the five activities is important. A strenuous relay practice should be followed by a less physically demanding throw or jump which can be followed by a second running activity which can be followed by a jump or a throw. Two running activities should never follow each other.

A typical rotation might be:

(1) Timed 50 m sprint.
(2) Throwing a netball.
(3) Shuttle relay, 30 m.
(4) Measured standing long jump.
(5) Throwing a hoop before rotating on to activity number 1.

Relays are the exciting climax of the lesson and should never be missed out. Many a lack-lustre lesson has come alive only during the relays when everyone gives their total attention and vocal encouragement to team mates, all really trying their hardest.

To enable him or her to praise progress, the teacher should time the winning team, and try to allow time for two or three races.

If the relay is similar to one practised in the group-work it reduces explanation time and gives more time for repeat races.

'Shall we have another one?' is always answered with 'Yes please!'

Relays are always a team activity, usually the whole group of six, and occasionally two partners. This allows slower runners the opportunity to be part of a winning team if all try hard. When the groups of six are formed at the start of the athletic activities programme, the teacher should aim for a good mix of boys and girls in each team and a good mix of sprinting ability so that the relays are always exciting and unpredictable.

Relays include:

(a) Partners, to line and back
    Line 1 | X1 X2 | Line 2
1 races to touch Line 1, turns, races back to touch stationary 2's hand.
2 races to touch Line 2, turns, races back to finish, standing beside partner.

(b) Shuttle relay
    X5 X3 X1 | | X2 X4 X6
1 races to pass baton to 2 and stays at back of 2's line. 2 races to give baton to 3 and stays at the back of 3's line. All 6 runners race to pass baton and stay at end of line, twice, thus finishing back in starting places. Race ends with 1 receiving the baton.

(c) End line to end line relay
    Line 1| X1 X2 X3 X4 X5 X6 | Line 2
1 races to touch Line 1, turns and races past team on team's right hand side to touch Line 2. 1 now turns and races back to give baton to 2, who repeats it all. All do the same with baton being passed to receiver on team's right. Race ends when baton is passed back to 1.

(d) End line and back relay, in teams of three
    X1 | X2 | X3 | | End line
1 races to pass baton to 2 who races to pass it to 3. 3 races to touch end line, turns and races to pass baton to 2 who races to pass it to 1 who races to finish at start line.

(e) Round track on field or circuit on playground.
Five 1s start at the same place on the track, and each runner covers one sixth of the race. On playground, teams use both netball courts and runners have spaced-apart starting places to run around their own netball court. Race ends with baton back to 1 at starting place.

TEACHING THE ATHLETIC ACTIVITIES LESSON

As in all areas of good physical education teaching, the teacher will see him or herself as a 'purveyor of action whose lessons are scenes of busy activity'. Over-long explanations; over-long demonstrations; too many stoppages; poor, slow responses by pupils in moving from activity to activity; bad behaviour or chattering among children, necessitating the repetition of explanations, must all be shunned and avoided in pursuit of lessons that are filled with almost non-stop, uninterrupted activity.

Familiarity with a lesson pattern by the pupils helps to speed up everything. Knowing and moving quickly into your own group places for warm-ups, timed lap on field or circuit runs on playground, group activities and end of lesson relays, speeds up the organisation – particularly if the teacher refuses to accept a slow response. 'Groups two and four, that was a really slow change-over. Go back to where you were and next time, be in place before I count to five. Move yourselves, go! One, two, three, four...well done! Always move like that in future so that we have a good lesson with plenty of time for everything.'

When the class is standing, listening to and looking at the teacher, he or she should stand still, and if the sun is shining, facing the sunshine, with the sun behind the pupils.

Particularly on the smaller area of the playground, most of the teaching and coaching will be from the outside of the rectangle, looking in, so that no-one is behind the teacher's back, out of sight and unsupervised. On the larger field 'classroom', such an 'outside looking in' approach is difficult to achieve. The teacher will usually take the shortest, inside route from group activity to adjacent activity to observe, comment, teach, coach and praise.

The observant teacher will endeavour to keep contact with all groups from whichever group he or she happens to be visiting. The usual form of contact will be an enthusiastic word of praise which uplifts the performer and informs the rest of the group. 'What a brilliant 50 metres sprint, Gary, really driving your arms and legs.' 'A very nice, smooth high jump, Sarah. I like your springy rock up into take-off, and your high swing of leading leg.' 'Andrew, your leading leg in hurdling is going straight up and over and down beautifully.'

When a demonstration is planned it can be speeded up by telling the demonstrators beforehand that they will be performing, and what they will be showing. 'In a minute, Rosie and Daniel, I am going to ask you to show your excellent tennis ball throwing. Please keep emphasising your side-on position, and your high arm bending to come over the shoulder.'

Because physical education lessons are so visual with pupils observed from a distance, the enthusiastic teacher can be almost continuously commenting on the many good things being seen. 'These lessons in the fresh air are good for you; they are good fun and exciting with lots of friendly competition; and your improvements and your friends' improvements give you plenty to feel pleased about.'

A PATTERN FOR TEACHING AN ATHLETIC ACTIVITIES SKILL

Relay baton exchange, as an example.

(1) Into positions quickly

With as few words as possible, explain the organisation and the starting positions. 'Partner 1, collect a baton and stand on this line. Partner 2, stand in front of your partner, in line with the two marker cones. Let me see how quickly you can be ready…go!'

(2) Into action quickly

With few words, the action is clearly explained, and can be demonstrated by the teacher and one pupil. 'I carry the baton in my left hand, run forward and bring it up into my partner's right hand. My partner receives it, standing still, then runs to cross the next line marked by cones. All ready, half-speed running up to partner, and a careful - changeover…go!'

(3) Emphasise main point to plan in your practice

'Partner 2, with baton now, stand ready to repeat the practice. You carry in your left hand and number one receives in the right hand, extended well back. Number two, bring it up into the inverted V of thumb and first finger. Number one, hold your hand back and still, with a good V for your partner to aim into. Ready. Half-speed running…go!'

(4) Further focused practice

'Let's have one more practice both ways. Receiver, stand facing the direction you are running, looking back over your right shoulder, and reaching back with a still right hand with its upside down V. (Thumb in, fingers out.) Number one, carry the baton in your left hand and sweep it up into the V.'

(5) Develop the technique

'We now want to receive the baton, slowly, on the move. Receiver, take care not to start moving too early or your partner might not catch up with you! Practise freely, both ways, aiming to receive the baton on the move at about half speed.'

(6) Demonstrations, observations, class comments

'Stop everyone and look at Adam and Laura who are doing this well. Watch them, then tell me what you thought was good about their performance.' (e. g. 'The receiver moves slowly into running at just the right time.' 'Receiver's right hand is still, with a good V and an easy target for the first partner.' 'Passer is bringing the baton up cleanly into the inverted V each time.')

(7) Thanks for demonstrations and helpful comments, then further class practice, planning to include some of the good things seen

'Remember that we are trying to keep the baton going, non-stop from start to finish. If the receiver says to him or herself "I am running, running, reaching, taking", that is a good guide to taking the baton, moving quite quickly. Receivers, experiment to check when to start running as your partner passes a check mark on the ground about 4 metres behind where you are standing now.'

(8) Finish with races

Partners now move on from their practising to the real thing, racing against all other couples.

NATIONAL CURRICULUM REQUIREMENTS FOR ATHLETIC ACTIVITIES

Key Stage 2: the main features

(1) A DUAL EMPHASIS — Performing and Learning

- **Planning**
Pupils are challenged to plan their actions and responses thoughtfully.
- **Performing**
Pupils are encouraged to work in a focused way, concentrating on the main feature of the task.

- **Reflecting and Evaluating**
Pupils are assisted to improve and progress as they adapt, develop, change and plan again, guided by their own and others' judgements.

(2) REQUIRED ACTIVITIES — Programme of Study

Pupils should be taught to:
(a) take part in and design challenges and competitions that call for precision, speed, power or stamina

(b) use running, jumping and throwing skills both singly and in combination
(c) pace themselves in these challenges and competitions.

(3) ATTAINMENT TARGET

By the end of the key stage, the majority of pupils should be able to demonstrate sufficient knowledge, skill and understanding to be able to:
(a) link skills, techniques and ideas and be able to apply them accurately and appropriately
(b) perform with precision, control and fluency
(c) compare and comment on skills, techniques and ideas used in own and others' work, and use this understanding to improve their performance
(d) explain and apply safety principles in preparing for exercise
(e) describe what effects exercise has on their bodies, and how it is valuable to their fitness and health.

(4) 'GOOD PRACTICE' POINTS TO NOTE

(a) In every lesson, most of the children's learning should take place through physical activity.
(b) Children should be given opportunities to practise, repeat and refine the skills they learn.
(c) Activities should be varied so that children do not become too tired in any one activity.
(d) There should be a range of competitions for individuals and groups.
(e) Children should set their own targets for performance and be given opportunities to measure and record throwing and jumping activities.
(f) Pupils should see good quality performances by their peers and others, and be encouraged to look at how movements start and finish.
(g) Pupils should receive specific guidance on skills, as well as general feedback and praise.
(h) Provide opportunities for pupils to talk about what they are doing, and comment on own and others' performances.

Self-critical reflection to check on the main features of physical education teaching within the National Curriculum usually requires answers to the following three questions:

(1) Was the class challenged to *plan* their actions in a focused, thoughtful way?
(2) Did the class spend most of the lesson time *performing*, doing, and being active in an enthusiastic, quiet and efficient way?
(3) Did the class have opportunities to observe, *reflect*, comment and make judgements on what they and others were doing? Did they then make practical use of such reflection to improve?

Planning

Because most teaching of athletic activities is teacher-centred to ensure a safe, correct way to perform, there are fewer opportunities for planning than, for example, in a dance lesson, where thirty widely different planned responses are expected.

In athletic activities there is much of 'Jump (or run, or throw, or hurdle) this way because it is efficient, neat, safe, correct.' Planning becomes more concerned with focusing on and trying to perform the salient points highlighted by the teacher, or observed in a good demonstration, and less concerned with improvised ways to perform.

Performing

As in all physical education activities, performing is, first, foremost and at all times, the most important element which must be enthusiastically pursued and taught by the teacher.

Lesson 'dead spots' – when nothing purposeful is happening – must be recognised and eliminated. They occur when bad behaviour causes the class to stand still, doing nothing while the teacher deals with the problem; when groups move far too slowly to their next place or activity, often talking and taking 30 seconds instead of a running 5 or 6 seconds; or every time the class needs to have something repeated because they are not listening.

In a well-ordered lesson with a well-behaved class, 25 of the 30 minutes can be spent working. The remaining 5 minutes, only, will be spent watching, listening or rotating from group to group.

Reflection/Evaluation

Because they are time consuming if overdone, demonstrations, observations, comments and judgements must be used sparingly and must be purposeful to bring about greater understanding and to show good quality work.

Reflection can be inspired by the teacher questioning:

'Jason, why did your front foot hit the hurdle?' (Took off too near.)

'Meena, how could you stand so that you could make a better throw with the netball?' (One foot in front of the other.)

'Steven, what things are important in good running?' (Straight ahead action, good heels, knees and arm uplift.)

Athletics coaches have long believed that recording results has a positive effect on overall achievement and enjoyment, as the following quotes demonstrate.

'If performance is constantly recorded, improvement will act as a spur to further effort';

'Athletics must be treated as a series of simple objective tests, and every opportunity must be taken to allow children to test themselves';

'A large proportion of class time must be spent in competitions of various types, with pupils measuring the performance of themselves and classmates'.

Personal score cards, made of card, should be made to keep a record of each pupil's achievement and progress.

If these are stored in an A4 plastic envelope, they will last for the whole of the year's athletic activities programme. Knowing that results are being recorded, and wanting to make an improvement, are spurs to continued effort. Without such recording some of the throwing, jumping and strenuous running activities might not be so industriously performed.

- Personal score cards will never leave the classroom. Pupils will have to remember the results of the two or three activities in which they were precisely timed or measured and then record their results back in class.
- Records of performances achieved during the first lessons of a series will enable the teacher to make any adjustments to the teams of six to make them more evenly matched.

- A team competition lesson can be included about once every five weeks to provide excitement, variety, and a different kind of competition to the more usual individual one, and to inspire a good group feeling. Six individuals become one united team.
- Each team has its recording card on the field or playground.
- The team leader will ask his team for their results and fill them in after each activity. 'Team four, give me your times for the lap, please… 1: 39 seconds; 2: 43; 3: 47; 4: 35; 5: 45; my number 6 time was 37. Our team total is 246 seconds. Well done, team four!'
- While the class is changing after the lesson the teacher can quickly work out the overall team positions in the 4–6 different activities contested during the competition. Evenly matched teams should have the pleasure of hearing that they achieved a good first, second or third place result in at least one of the events.
- From the team score cards individuals can transfer their results on to their individual score cards.
- With repeated practice, improved technique and the spur of competition, improvement and progress in running, jumping and throwing are greater than in any other area of physical education – and, ideally, the development will have been written down as proof.
- As sprint, lap or circuit times tumble, and as throwing and jumping distances expand, pupils become fitter, stronger, more versatile and skilful. It is hoped that they will also feel more self-assured and confident.

Individual score card of times, distances, heights

Name _____   Class _____

Events	September	April	May	June	July
Running					
50 m					
75 m					
100 m					
150 m					
200 m					
250 m					
300 m					
Throwing					
Tennis ball					
Large ball					
Bean bag put					
Hoop					
Quoit					
Jumping					
High					
Long					
Triple					
Standing high					
Standing long					

SAFE PRACTICE AND ACCIDENT PREVENTION

Unlike the secondary school athletic activities lesson with its shot, discus and javelin throwing, the junior school lesson is not a high-risk occasion. However, as in all physical education lessons where pupils are moving about quickly in continuous close proximity to one another, we must do everything possible to ensure safety and accident prevention.

A safe environment requires:

(1) A quiet, attentive, well behaved class which responds readily and immediately to instructions. For example, if the class is practising an easy, 3-step scissors jump over a cane held low by a partner, at about knee height, there will be no accidents if the class follow instructions. If the partner wrongly holds the cane up high, at about waist height, and if the runner charges in at full speed with ten or more steps, there will be an accident with the jumper landing awkwardly, particularly from a grass take-off or a slippy, gritty take-off on the playground.

(2) Good supervision by the teacher, who is always aware of how the whole class is responding, particularly when the five different groups are practising. For example, if a group is practising shuttle relays, the baton should be carried and received with the right hand so that the first runner in lane one hands the baton to the second runner in lane two. Only by doing this can we ensure that one runner does not crash into another of the same team in the same lane, or worse, push the baton into the receiver's tummy when they fail to make a good hand to hand change-over.

(3) Good teaching to develop the correct way to lift, carry and use equipment safely. For example, 'You are going to a large space to practise a 3-step scissors jump over a low cane held by your partner. When you collect the cane, carry it in front of you, vertically. Never hold it horizontally over a shoulder, which would be at eye level of someone, unseen, behind you.'

The 1-metre canes, held by a partner and used for standing high jump or scissors jump, should have their ends taped so that they are smooth, round and safe. A cork from a wine bottle is an excellent end piece for preventing accidents from canes that might be kicked from someone's hand or struck by a leg when being used as a hurdle.

(4) Good teaching that promotes the safe practising of skills. 'In the hoop throwing group, I want Susan to check that the three throwers are all on the marked line; 3 metres apart; side on to the direction you are throwing; waiting to hear Susan's command, 'Ready…swing back…throw!', for your round body, slinging action throw. You are aiming to release it straight forward. When all the hoops have landed, your partners will mark the distances and then change places with you; still being organised by Susan this week.'

(5) Awareness of the safety risks of wearing inappropriate clothing, footwear and jewellery. Watches, rings and jewellery worn by a runner, thrower or jumper can strike against another standing or performing near, and cause serious scarring and injury.

(6) The whole-body warming-up activities are essential to stimulate the body systems which have only been ticking over gently if the class has been sedentary in the previous lesson.

An example of a track and field layout for athletic activities

Five group activities in any one lesson include at least one jumping activity. The scaled-down, half-speed, safe, long, high and triple jumping practices do not need any permanent field markings. It is assumed that the field is not provided with proper landing facilities for optimum effort jumping.

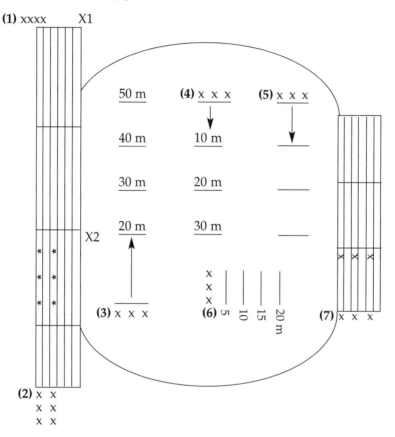

The one or two running, activities, including hurdles and relays, and the one or two throws to be included in a lesson can be chosen from the following.

(1) 50-m sprint. X1 is runner. X2 is starter/timekeeper.

(2) Hurdling over 3 sets of canes on pairs of cones. (* denotes cone.)

(3) Tennis ball throwing. Partner marks and measures best of three throws.

(4) Hoop throwing. Partner marks and measures best of three throws.

(5) Large-ball throw. Partner marks and measures best of three throws.

(6) Bean bag put. Partner marks and measures best of three throws.

(7) Relay baton exchange practice within 20 m area.

THE PLAYGROUND ATHLETIC ACTIVITIES 'CLASSROOM'

The dimensions given below, for a typical two-netball-courts area, are ideal for the lessons that follow as they give an exact 150- and 300-m circuit around the outside of the two courts.

If a school is having its faint lines repainted, these dimensions are worth considering. A short start/finish line for the two distances can be painted at right angles to the most appropriate end or side line where there is good space for the whole class to gather for the start and congregate at the finish. The run in at the end should also be well clear of fences, hutted classrooms or school walls so that runners can 'Finish fast!' in safety.

The extra 50- and 100-m distances, to provide finishes for 200- and 250-m circuits, can be measured with a wheel and marked with a line at right angles to the end or side line concerned.

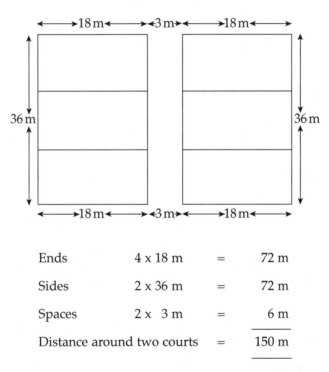

Ends	4 x 18 m	=	72 m
Sides	2 x 36 m	=	72 m
Spaces	2 x 3 m	=	6 m
Distance around two courts		=	150 m

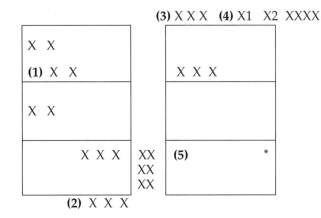

(1) 3-step scissors jump over low cane held by partner.

(2) Relays up and down court, using middle third of court as baton exchange, in both directions.

(3) Bean bag put from end line with partner marking and measuring the best of 3 puts.

(4) 50-m timed sprint around cone (*) at 25 metres. X1 is taking his or her turn as time-keeper, X2 as sprinter.

(5) Standing long jump with a partner, across width of court.

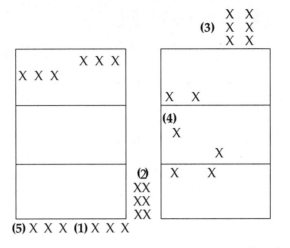

(1) Tennis-ball throw, end to end, to be measured by partner.

(2) Partners, standing long jump across width of court.

(3) Hurdling down one of two lanes of three 'hurdles', canes on cones.

(4) Two sets of partners try to throw large ball to each other over heads of third couple in middle, trying to catch it.

(5) How far can you run in 5 seconds? One partner is challenged to tell marking partner where to stand as estimate of 5 seconds run. Runners sprint for 5 seconds and partners mark the actual distance – always far less than estimated.

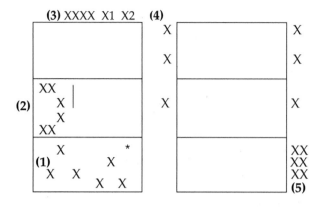

(1) Two trios in a 4-m-sided triangle. Pass and run practice.

(2) Scissors high jump over low elastic 'bar' tied between high jump stands. 3-stride approach only, for safety.

(3) 50 metre timed sprint around cone (*) at 25 metres. X1 is taking his or her turn at time-keeping. X2 is sprinting.

(4) Throwing hoop for accuracy and medium distance across width of court, with a partner.

(5) Partner fun runs across width of court. (Fun runs are simple, novelty, competitive races over a very short distance.)

LESSON PLAN • 30–50 MINUTES

WARM-UP ACTIVITIES   4–6 minutes

(1) Show me your best running, visiting all parts of the playground 'classroom'. Can you lift heels and knees to run so quietly that I wouldn't know you were there if I closed my eyes?

(2) Can you use the lines to show me long and high jumps as you find out which is your jumping foot for long and high jumps?

TIMED PART CIRCUIT OF 100 METRES   4–6 minutes

(1) Groups one and two will go off first and complete their run. Then groups three and four will do their run. Finally, group five will go. Please remember your starting time and your finishing time. To work out your time for 100 metres, you subtract start time from finish time.

(2) Run outside lines of both netball courts. 'Group one, zero seconds, go! Group two, ten seconds, go!'

CLASS ACTIVITIES   18–32 minutes

Whole class tennis ball throw with a partner.
(1) Stand, 3–4 metres apart and throw underarm for an easy catch.
(2) Put one foot forward for balance. Hold cupped hands forward as a target for partner to aim at.
(3) Swing arm forward, back, then forward into your aim and throw.
(4) One of you stay on this side line while the other partner, step by step, moves back until you both need to start throwing overarm. Then do not move any further apart.
(5) In overarm throwing, stand side-on to your partner, with rear leg bent and throwing arm well back. Throw by bending and bringing arm over shoulder before straightening it into the throw.

Whole class relay race with a partner.
(1) Stand, side by side, between the side lines of the netball court, not too near other couples.
(2) Number one will race to touch side line on your side, then race back to touch partner who races to side line on the other side of the playground. Partner races back to stand still beside you. Ready, number ones? Go! (Teacher calls out results.)
(3) Well done. Let's have another race. This time, speed it up by jumping into your turn at the side line and number two, you can crouch, ready, with knees bent to give an explosive send-off. Go!
(4) For our last race, let's have number two starting. Show me your quick turns at the line, and your crouching, ready start, number ones, as you wait for the hand touch. Go!

TEAM SHUTTLE RELAYS   4–6 minutes

X5 X3 X1 | | X2 X 4 X6

1 races with baton to give it to 2, and stays at the end of that opposite line.
2 races to give baton to 3 and stays at the end of that line.

3 to 4 to 5 to 6 and all have changed sides.
Race continues until all are back in starting places with last runner, 6, giving baton to 1.
Baton is carried and received in right hand to avoid spearing receiver.

The lesson's main emphases include

(a) Training the class to respond quickly to instructions; to be physically active; and to cooperate wholeheartedly in pursuit of a lesson that flows, almost non-stop, from start to finish.

(b) Introducing the class to what, for them, is a new kind of lesson with its running, jumping, throwing and relays.

Equipment needed

- 15 tennis balls
- 15 batons
- marker cones for pupils to run around in the timed circuit

Warm-up activities

(1) The limits to their running are explained as the area within the netball courts. 'Wanderers' have to be told to 'Stay inside our playground classroom area'. Good running, they are told, is 'quiet and you do not follow anyone. Run on straight lines, not curving in a big circle, all following one another.'

(2) Long jumping, with a long reaching front leg, is from one of the many lines. High jumping with a leading leg bending to reach up high, can be straight over or from an angle over one of the lines.

Timed circuit

(1) The exact route of the circuit is explained. 'Outside the six marker cones – no cutting corners!' In case of mathematical inadequacy, most have only to remember their finish time. Two groups have to subtract 10 seconds from finish time.

(2) 'Finish running fast past the last cone.' is requested to counteract any deceleration as they come to the line. When finished, runners are asked to confirm that they know their exact times for recording back in class.

Class activities

Easy to teach since all are working at the same activity. Five different group activities, all at the same time, and the eventual pattern for this main part of the lesson, are, however, difficult to organise, control and teach in a first lesson.

In the throwing activity, one line of throwers will be well spaced along the whole length of a netball court side line. Their partners will gradually move back until they are near the opposite side line for the overarm throwing. A demonstration by competent couples will show good style overarm throwing and good, two-handed catching, and be more valuable than trying to explain all the elements of 'arm bending to come high over your shoulder, then stretch into the aim and throw, with a long follow-through of arm'.

In the whole class relay, from being side by side, down the centre of the playground, each has to run to touch the nearer side line with a foot, then race back to touch partner's outstretched hand.

Teacher stands at one end of long line to watch and call out names of as many couples as possible, as they finish, and to see if any are not playing fairly, either by missing the line or going before being touched.

Team shuttle relays

If halves of teams are slightly offset to the left, the baton will be passed safely, right hand to right hand, with no possibility of spearing the receiver's tummy.

LESSON PLAN • 30–50 MINUTES

WARM-UP ACTIVITIES   3–4 minutes

(1) Follow your leader who will show you two or three athletic actions – walking; running; jumping; hurdling; triple jumping.

(2) When you can repeat the leader's sequence, become the new leader. Join actions smoothly.

TIMED CIRCUIT OR PART CIRCUIT OF 100 METRES   3–5 minutes

(1) Keep outside the marker cones. Race past the finish, listening for your time. Subtract starting time from finishing time.
(2) In the first run, groups one to three only.

Groups four and five will be in a separate, second run. 'Group one, zero seconds, go! Group two, five seconds, go! Group three, ten seconds, go!'

CLASS ACTIVITY; Bean bag throw to partner   5–8 minutes

(1) Partner with bean bag, stand on this side line, well spaced apart from other couples. Other partner, stand 3–4 metres away, with hands well forward, cupped to receive the bean bag.
(2) Catching is important. Watch it all the way into your hands.
(3) When throwing, swing arm forward, back, then forward into aim and smooth throw. Partner's

hands are held still as a good target to aim at.
(4) Partner, not on line, move back a step at a time, until you need to start throwing overarm, then do not move any more. Throw side-on and overarm, bending arm high over shoulder.
(5) Start with arm well back, feet wide apart. Can you feel your back leg push; your upper body turn; then the arm bending into the throw?

GROUP ACTIVITIES; Five groups of six   16–28 minutes

(1) Bean bag throw into a hoop on the ground at 4–5 metres. Each partner has 3 bean bags and competes against own partner.
(2) Timed 50-metre sprint from a starting line to run around a cone at 25 metres and back to the starting line where the timekeeper/starter stands. Each has a turn at starting/timing.
(3) Scissors high jump over cane held low by partner. A 3-step run in at an angle to the cane starts with foot that is also the take-off foot. Partner checks that leg nearer cane swings up.

(4) Rugby ball pass and follow across 3 metres. Group is divided into two trios.

    X3 X1 | | X2

1 passes to 2 and runs to end of opposite line. 2 passes to 3 and runs to end of opposite line, and so on until all are back in own start places. Practise, then challenge other trio to a race.
(5) Fun races across width of court, each member taking a turn as starter: (a) quick walking, (b) hop half way on one foot, then use other foot, (c) sprinting, (d) skipping with rope, (e) invent a race.

SIDE-TO-SIDE RELAY RACES WITH A PARTNER   3–5 minutes

Partners stand, side by side, down middle of playground, equidistant from side lines of netball courts.
1 races to touch nearer side line, and races back to touch partner's outstretched hand.

2 repeats it to own, nearer side line and races back to finish beside partner.
Teacher calls out results and times winners.
Race again, with each partner starting, looking for improved times.

LESSON NOTES • 3 LESSONS DEVELOPMENT

The lesson's main emphases include

(a) Promoting safe practice through appropriate dress; immediate responses; sharing space co-operatively; good behaviour.

(b) Throwing for accuracy and working safely, alone, in pairs and in a group.

Equipment needed

- 6 skipping ropes
- 15 bean bags
- 3 canes
- 2 rugby balls
- marker cones for circuit
- stopwatch

Warm-up activities

(1) The linking movements will be jogging or running between the athletic activities, i.e., run and jump high; run and jump long; run and hurdle; run into hop, step and jump.
(2) Encourage a varied trio of activities, e.g. quick walking; run and jump high; run and hurdle.

Timed circuit

(1) No cutting corners! There are many corners when you are on a playground circuit, but the distance is measured to the outside of lines we run around. Keep outside our playground class-room, now!
(2) Groups one to three will run first and be timed, then groups four and five will go. Listen carefully for start and finish times. You work out your circuit times by subtracting start times from finish times. Group one, zero seconds, go! Group two, five seconds, go! (etc.)

Class activity

Catching a bean bag is easier than catching a ball because the bean bag does not bounce away. Almost non-stop throwing and catching practice can be achieved. Their overarm throw-and-catch distance is near enough for accuracy, but far enough to need a correct, side-on starting position. Look out for and demonstrate good examples of: wide, side-on stance with arm well back; rear leg drive; upper body turn; arm bending high over shoulder before stretching into throw.

Group activities

(1) After practising the aiming/throwing action successfully, they can compete against own partner in a 'best of three' throws, or pairs can compete against other pairs, in a 'best of six' throws.
(2) Teacher explains how to start, stop and read the stopwatch, and how to start a run 'Set…go!' Timekeeper tells runner his or her time, then gives them the watch to start and time next runner.
(3) Cane is low at about 45 cm and held loosely so that it is not impeding the jumper. They work out the side from which to run in at a 45-degree angle. Jumping foot is the one remote from cane.
(4) Rugby ball pass and follow is like the shuttle relay of September, passing and following to run to the end of the opposite line. Trios can race to make 12 pass and follows.
(5) Short fun runs with a moment's breather in between races. Each has turn at 'Set…go!' or one can be starter/judge, each time.

Side to side relays with a partner

Races are made more interesting if timed by teacher. Times are improved by a jumping turn at the line, landing crouched, ready to sprint back to touch partner who should be in a crouched position, ready to speed away. First to fifth results are called out by teacher.

LESSON PLAN • 30–50 MINUTES

WARM-UP ACTIVITIES   3–4 minutes

(1) Group one leading, walk to first line across netball court, thinking 'straight ahead' travel action with arms swinging straight forward and back. Jog to second line, legs and arms moving straight ahead. Run to cross end line, again with emphasis on straight ahead arms, legs and shoulders.
(2) Return down adjacent court, walking, jogging and running again. Pretend that you are travelling down a narrow alley, having to keep straight ahead to avoid bumping the walls. Go!

TIMED CIRCUIT OF 150 METRES   4–5 minutes

(1) Our track or circuit has sharp corners, all marked by cones for you to go round. Aim to keep running at a steady rhythm.
(2) Groups five to three will go first and be timed, then groups two and one. Listen for your starting time which you subtract from your finishing time. Group five, no seconds, go.

CLASS ACTIVITY; 3-steps scissors jump over low cane   5–8 minutes

(1) Partner with cane, find a good space for your partner to work in easily and safely. Hold your cane low at about knee height.
(2) Have four or five turns each, taking only a 3 step run in. Start with the foot that is also your jumping off foot. Left, right, left, or right, left , right. Come in at a 45-degree angle.
(3) Watching partner, check that the jumper is jumping with the foot further from the cane, and swinging up the leg nearer the cane.

GROUP ACTIVITIES; Five groups of six   15–28 minutes

(1) 3-steps scissors jump over low cane held by partner. Six turns each, running in to jump from both sides on the 45 degree line. Slow, springy run up for a safe, controlled jump and landing.
(2) Partners relay down length of one side of netball court. 1s race from end line to pass baton to 2s at middle of court. 2s race to cross end line first, then have a few seconds rest, turn around and repeat back to start, racing other couples.
(3) Bean bag put with a partner from an end line of court. Each has three puts with partner marking best with a dome cone. From a side-on position with feet wide, and with a bean bag against neck, they feel a rear leg drive, an upper body rotation, then the push of the bag straight forward from the neck, with explosive arm push.
(4) 50-metre timed sprint around a cone at 25 metres and back to line of starter/timekeeper. Each takes turn, starting and timing one runner; telling runner the time; then having own run.
(5) Partners, standing long jump, to cross width of court. 1 does a standing long jump from side line and stands still. 2 does the next jump from line of toes of 1's landing place. They jump alternately to see how many jumps are needed to take them across.

SIX IN A LINE RELAY   3–5 minutes

Line 1 | X1 X2 X3 X4 X5 X6 | Line 2
1 races to touch Line 1, turns, races past team to touch line 2, turns and races back to give baton to 2 who repeats it all. Race ends when baton is back with 1.

LESSON NOTES • 3 LESSONS DEVELOPMENT

The lesson's main emphases include

(a) Developing and refining basic techniques in running, jumping and throwing.
(b) Much partner activity which should lead to an appreciation of the big contribution a partner makes to learning athletic skills.

Equipment needed

- 15 canes
- 9 bean bags
- 5 batons
- stopwatch
- marker cones for timed runs and throws

Warm-up activities

(1) There is much wobbling from side to side among runners, losing forward distance with each zig-zag.

(2) From front view, the teacher can see the best 'straight ahead' actions, and demonstrate with them to explain his or her meaning and aim.

Timed circuit or circuit and part circuit

(1) Emphasise 'While we do our lesson inside the lines of the playground classroom, we run our circuit entirely outside that area. Do not take short-cuts.'
(2) Poor mathematicians may need help with the subtraction of starting times from finishing times.

Class activity

(1) A demonstration of an easy, slow, safe, 3-counts approach – straight away by the teacher, or very soon by a pupil – is essential to show what is wanted.

(2) Partner holds cane gently so that, if struck, it does not knock the jumper off balance.
(3) Legs swing up one after the other, then land one after the other.

Group activities

Groups of six allow partner-work in five groups.
(1) After landing, you can stay where you are, turn around, move back to your 3-strides distance from the cane, and come in again.
(2) First runner, with baton in left hand, races to give baton to a stationary 2's right hand, held straight back with an inverted V between thumb in and fingers out. One of group acts as starter.
(3) Teacher demonstrates the bean bag tight into neck position, and explains that any movement backwards by the bag and hand from the neck is a throw, not a put, and is not allowed. The hand drives forward at about 60 degrees, and there is a final flick with the wrist.
(4) Runner starts in a slightly crouched, sprint start position, one leg and arm forward, ready to drive off. Short rapid strides take you around the 25-metre marker cone. Finish fast past the line.
(5) In a standing long jump, start with feet slightly apart. Arms swing up above head, then swing down behind you as the knees bend. Legs drive forwards into leap with a strong throw forward of arms. Land with strong pull forward of both feet.

Six in a line relay

Lines 1 and 2 are the end lines of a netball court, with teams lined up in the middle third of the court. Baton is carried in left hand for passing to right hand of next runner who is stationary, showing a good, inverted V between thumb and first finger. Runners travel on right side of team, with next runner stepping out to right to wait. Runner swaps baton from right hand to left for the next change-over.

Results and times should be called out after each of the two or three races have been contested.

LESSON PLAN • 30–50 MINUTES

WARM-UP ACTIVITIES   3–4 minutes

(1) Groups line up across end line and jog to first line of court; run with good lift of heels, knees and arms to finish fast, crossing second line; then slow down to end line and turn around.

(2) Same again, back to start, jogging then finishing fast. Good knee and heel lift aims to give you a longer stride, moving you further forward with each stride. Lift and reach with leg.

TIMED CIRCUIT OF 150 METRES   4–5 minutes

(1) This is a timed circuit run for you, not a race against others. Keep to a sensible, less than sprinting rhythm and finish feeling fit to carry on with the rest of the lesson.

(2) Stand, ready to go off at 5 second intervals. Listen for, and remember your start and finish times. Group one, zero seconds, go! Group two, five seconds, go! (etc.)

CLASS ACTIVITY; Relay baton exchange   5–8 minutes

(1) Partner with baton, stand on this end line, baton in left hand. Other partner, on the first line, right hand back with an inverted V between thumb and fingers, for partner to aim at.
(2) 1s, jog and give baton to partner. 2s, jog to next line, stop and turn around for next practice,

with baton in left hand.
(3) Well done. This time, take the baton, moving slowly forward to keep it just moving from start to finish. Receiver, start going off as partner passes a mark on the ground about 4 metres behind you (Several practices both ways to check the marks.)

GROUP ACTIVITIES; Five groups of six   15–28 minutes

(1) Baton exchange practices with partner, down length of court, with partner receiving between first and second lines on the move, and running at speed to cross end line. After several practices, race other couples to finish fast and finish first.
(2) Large ball throw from a side line. Partner, 10–15 metres away on court, marks best throw (where ball lands, not where it rolls to) with dome cone. Ball is thrown with straight arms from above and behind head.
(3) High jump, scissors action over low elastic 'bar' tied between jumping stands. A slow, bouncy, 3-

step approach from 45 degrees is used. Take off and landing are totally scaled down for safety.
(4) 50 metres timed sprint around a cone at 25 metres and back. Only one runner at a time is started and timed by one of the group.
(5) Tennis-ball throw for accuracy, in threes. Hoop is held high by one and the other two aim to throw ball through hoop to each other for an easy catch. Rotate after six attempts and compete against other trio for 'best of 18 throws.' Throw 3 metres from hoop.

SHUTTLE RELAYS; 30 metres   3–5 minutes

```
   X5 X3 X1 |              | X2 X4 X6
```
1 races to hand baton (right hand to right hand) to 2, and stays at back of opposite line. 2 races to give baton to 3, and 2 stays at back of opposite

line. This continues until all race back to own side and race ends with 5 handing baton to 1. Two races will be run and timed, with results called out by teacher, first to fifth.

The lesson's main emphases include

(a) Demonstrating when asked; looking at demonstrations; making friendly, helpful comments about the work seen.
(b) Refining basic techniques in running, jumping, and throwing for distance and accuracy.
(c) Sustaining energetic activity and feeling what happens to our body during exercise.

Equipment needed

- 15 batons
- 3 large balls
- 2 tennis balls
- measuring tape
- stopwatch
- high jump stands and elastic bar
- marker cones for circuit and throws

Warm-up activities

(1) Netball court is split handily into thirds by two lines across, giving walking, sprinting and slowing-down thirds of court.
(2) If you keep up same stride rhythm, but add, say, 10 cm to each stride, you are running faster. There should be an impression of lifting knees and heels and reaching forward with front foot.

Timed circuit

(1) This is not a race. It is a test of your ability to spread your effort sensibly over 150 metres and finish, still running, and able to recover quickly. Do not sprint off too quickly or you will finish feeling distressed, and too tired to continue.
(2) After your run I will ask you 'How do you feel? Do you know why you are hot and breathing deeply? And I will ask, as always, if you have managed to work out your circuit time, by subtracting start from finish time.'

Class activity

(1) Teacher demonstrates the inverted V between thumb and first finger of right hand, held still for easy baton exchange.
(2) A stationary change-over for the first practice lets both partners feel the correct action, up into the V, with receiver passive.
(3) 'Mark on ground' can be a small stone, weed, bare patch or long piece of grass. Teacher can demonstrate a 'slowly moving forward' change-over, pointing out and watching the check mark and responding to the incoming runner crossing it.

Group activities

(1) Partners practise baton exchange with receiver saying 'Running, running, reaching, taking' after partner crosses check mark.
(2) Each has three throws from a side line, one foot in front of the other for good balance and to help powerful arm-swing forward.
(3) Low elastic 'bar' gives if you hit it, saving time and preventing painful shins. Jump is not high, but style can still be good, with long swing up and over of leading leg.
(4) Ensure that there is space for a good run-in past the timekeeper if they are to 'finish fast, running across line' with safety.
(5) Because the distance is short, you can throw underarm as you aim at the high hoop. Swing throwing arm forward, back and then forward into aim and throw.

Shuttle relays

Passing baton from right hand to right hand is helped if teams are off-set, slightly to the left of each other, so that the baton never hits the receiving partner in the tummy if there is a fumble. The baton should be received, standing still at the line.

LESSON PLAN • 30–50 MINUTES

WARM-UP ACTIVITIES   3–4 minutes

(1) Jog, side by side, with your partner. One sets a steady, sensible rhythm that seems right for today's 200 metres circuit run.
(2) Other partner now sets rhythm, 'feeling' an easy speed to be kept up for the whole circuit.
(3) Have a short rest, then both have a go at setting the sensible, continuous, steady rhythm that you think will be suitable.

TIMED CIRCUIT AND PART CIRCUIT OF 200 METRES   4–5 minutes

(1) This is our longest timed run of the year. I want you to make a weekly improvement, so take your time and make sure that you use a speed that you know you can keep up. Be sensible!
(2) Let's start with number five group this month for a change. All listen for your starting and finishing times carefully.

CLASS ACTIVITY; Tennis ball throw   5–8 minutes

(1) One partner stands on the side line and the other stands about 4 metres away for an easy, two-handed catch.
(2) Catcher, hold both hands forward, cupped, to give your partner a target to aim at.
(3) Move apart until you need to start throwing overarm. Then don't move any further back. Stand side-on with throwing arm back.
(4) Throw by bending arm to bring it high over your shoulder into throw and follow-through.

GROUP ACTIVITIES; Five groups of six   15–28 minutes

(1) Tennis ball throwing across court, overarm, aiming to bounce ball into a hoop, half way across court, for partner to catch.
(2) Relay baton change-over. 1 runs to pass to 2 who uses middle third to get into running strides before receiving baton in right hand. 2 sprints past end line. Short rest and repeat with 2 starting this time.
(3) Measured standing long jump from part of a line. 2 metre sticks parallel with jumps give exact result. Each jumps, lands and stands still to be told distance by previous jumper at side.
(4) Careful hoop throw from end line to partner, standing 10–15 metres down court. Stand side-on to each other when throwing, discus style. Arm starts straight back, fingers over and thumb under grip. Rotation of upper body brings hoop around, shoulder high with straight arm, to front, head high.
(5) Fun runs from end line to second line down court. Each takes a turn at starting and judging: (a) quick walking (b) sprinting (c) skipping (d) bowling a hoop (e) invent a simple fun run.

ROUND THE NETBALL COURT RELAY   3–5 minutes

One netball court has three teams lined up at team starting places, well apart, on inside of line round court. The other court has two teams lined up. 1 stands, ready, on 'track' outside line. On teacher's 'Go!' 1 races once around own court and passes baton to 2 who has stepped out, ready to receive the baton in the right hand, on the move, from 1's left hand. Race ends with baton back in hand of 1, with teacher calling out the results and winner's time.

LESSON NOTES • 3 LESSONS DEVELOPMENT

The lesson's main emphases include

(a) Enjoying a varied, interesting and challenging lesson made almost non-stop by pupils' co-operation and responsiveness.

(b) Running over longer distances and measuring, comparing and improving own performances.

Equipment needed

- 15 tennis balls
- 9 hoops
- 6 skipping ropes
- 5 batons
- 2 metre sticks
- marker cones for relays and circuits

Warm-up activities

(1) Try to remember 150-metre rhythm of the previous lesson, and make this month's circuit running a bit slower. Keeping going is the main thing.

(2) The practising should at least deter pupils from starting off too quickly, as if it were a race.

Timed circuit and part circuit

(1) Runners will start at one place and, on most primary school playgrounds, be finishing at a point further on around the circuit where the timekeeping/judging teacher will then be standing. We want steadiness at start, middle and finish – not a quick dash start and a walking, weary finish.

(2) Groups line up, tucked in behind one another, to run as near to the line as possible, so that they are not running wide and further.

Class activity

(3&4) If necessary – with balls flying all over the place – the teacher will dominate the practice, and make the pupils throw to command. '1s, side-on, lean back and throw! 2s, let arm bend high over shoulder, ready, throw!'
A demonstration of good quality throwing is an invaluable aid.

Group activities

(1) Thrower still starts, side-on, with throwing arm high above shoulder, then bend-stretches into aim and throw at target hoop. Partners can compete against each other, or against the other two couples in their group. Best of six throws.

(2) First runner has baton in left hand. Receiving partner uses a check mark on ground, 4–5 metres behind him or her, as signal to start running, when partner passes it. Right arm is back and ready with inverted V of thumb and first finger ready to receive baton.

(3) In standing long jump, start with feet slightly apart. Swing arms high above head. Bend knees and swing arms down behind. Drive forward with legs and swing forward with both arms. Land by bending legs under you for maximum distance.

(4) Because of limited space on playground, this is a scaled-down throw, probably half of what many can do. The side-on, discus style, long arm slinging action is what we want, and a hoop flying flat so that it does not roll on landing.

(5) The starter/judge stands at line, two thirds down the netball court, from which they are started ('Set…go!') and judged.

Round netball court relays

Because of limited space outside netball courts on many playgrounds, it is not possible to have all five 1s in a relay starting at the same place. This race is one way of having the fun of a round-the-outside circuit relay with no team running wider and further than any other team. Two races are run, judged and timed.

Year 3 • Playground Team Competition

LESSON PLAN • 30-50 MINUTES

WARM-UP ACTIVITIES   3-4 minutes

(1) Jog easily, visiting all parts of the netball court. Can you let hands, arms and legs relax completely with no stiffness?
(2) Move a little faster now, with more uplift in heels, knees, arms, and reaching out further with your leading leg each time.
(3) On 'Stop!' (for moment's rest) let me see who is first to stand, balanced on tip toes on a line. Stop! (Repeat 2 and 3.)

TIMED CIRCUIT OF 150 METRES   3-5 minutes

To assist quick subtraction of starting time from finishing time to work out circuit time, two teams only at a time go off at no seconds and ten seconds, necessitating three groups of runners – groups one and two; three and four; and five by itself. All times are recorded for the competition.

GROUP ACTIVITIES; Five groups of six   20-35 minutes

(1) Timed 50-metre sprint around a cone at 25 metres and back. Each is started and timed individually by a team member.
(2) Measured team standing long jump from a line. Leader does a standing long jump and stands still. Next jumper stands in line with previous jumper's toes, does the next jump and stands still to let number three see where to start. Team result is marked and measured.
(3) Bean bag aiming into a hoop in threes (half teams), throwing from a line 5 metres away. Each team member has three throws and the scores are combined. The better of the two half-team scores is recorded.
(4) Non-scoring, throwing a tennis ball to land within lines of ropes to bounce and be caught by partner.

   X1 | 1 | 3 | 5 | 3 | 1 | X2

Each space between ropes has its value written in chalk. Three pairs take part and pairs can compete against other pairs.
(5) Large ball throw across court. Partner marks and measures to where ball landed. Each partner has three turns, then changes over. Long, two-handed throw with arms above and behind head.

TEAM SHUTTLE RELAYS   4-6 minutes

End Line 1   End Line 2
  | X1 X2 X3 X4 X5 X6 |

1 in each team races to touch end Line 1, turns and races back past team on their right to touch line 2, turns and races back to give baton to 2 who repeats it all. All do one run, end to end, and the race ends when baton is given to 1 by 6. Teacher calls out all results, first to fifth, for scoring purposes. Winner's time is recorded for future interest.

Team Number _____

First place in activity gains five points for a team. Fifth place gains one point.

Event	Individual Results						Combined Result	Place 1st–5th	Points 5–1
	1	2	3	4	5	6			
150 m									
50 m									
Team long jump									
Bean bag aim									
Large ball throw									
Shuttle relay									
								Total Points Position in Class	

LESSON PLAN • 30–50 MINUTES

WARM-UP ACTIVITIES   3–4 minutes

(1) One group at a time jogs to the first line, hits the line with one foot and then runs at speed to the second line, counting the number of strikes made by the starting foot to cross the area.

(2) This time, in your speed running, can you lift your heels and knees to give you a longer stride; count to see if you cross the middle third with fewer strides. Jog; sprint and count; jog. Go!

TIMED CIRCUIT OF 150 METRES   3–5 minutes

(1) Travel at something between the jog and the brisk run you have just practised, not slow marathon, not high-speed sprint.

(2) You will go off at 5 second intervals. Keep outside the marker cones and remember your start and finish times so that you can work out your circuit time. Group one, no seconds, go! (and so on to 'Group five, twenty seconds, go!')

CLASS ACTIVITY; Throwing large ball   5–8 minutes

(1) Partners stand 3–4 metres apart for an easy, two-handed pass from chest or from above one shoulder, aiming at partner's chest.

(2) Now stand about 12 metres apart for a longer throw with straight arms starting above and behind head. Place your feet one in front of other for balance. Your whole body comes into the powerful throw; make it accurate for an easy catch by your partner.

GROUP ACTIVITIES; Five groups of six   16–28 minutes

(1) Large ball pass from chest or shoulder, 3–4 metres away to bounce ball into hoop for partner to catch. Then move to double that distance for the longer, overhead throw straight to partner.

(2) Standing high jump over cane held by partner at about 45 cm. Jump from facing cane at arms length, or side-on close to cane. A good knees bend with swing back of arms is followed by a vigorous leg drive and swing up of arms. Have four turns and change

(3) 50-metre timed sprint around a cone at 25 metres and back. Each group member has turn at starting/timekeeping, telling runner his or her time, and being timed individually.

(4) Centre third of netball court is a good length for practising the baton exchange. Three pairs compete against each other. After racing in one direction to far line, they rest for a few seconds, then race back to final starting line. Baton is taken on the move in inverted V of right hand thumb and first finger.

(5) Partner fun runs across one third of the netball court and back to touch other partner who does the same in: (a) quick walks; (b) sprints; (c) huge bounding strides; (d) skipping; (e) own invented run.

SHUTTLE RELAYS; 30 metres apart   3–5 MINUTES

      X5 X3 X1 | | X2 X4 X6
1 races to give baton to 2 and stays at end of opposite line. 2 races to give baton to 3 and stays at end of opposite line. All race to end of opposite line, stay, then race back in opposite direction to end at own starting position. Race ends with 5 giving baton to leader 1. The baton is carried and received in the right hand. Ideally, teams are slightly off-set to the left of each other to help the baton exchange.

The lesson's main emphases include

(a) Establishing a tradition of immediate responses to instructions and wholehearted participation in vigorous physical activity.
(b) Encouraging pupil co-operation to let lesson flow, almost non-stop, from warm-up to finish.
(c) Refining the quality of techniques in running, jumping and throwing.

Equipment needed

- 15 large balls
- 15 cones
- 6 skipping ropes
- 5 batons
- marker cones for circuit and relays
- stopwatch

Warm-up activities

(1) The quick count needed is easier if done once in two strides. Double score to see how many strides needed.
(2) Value of knee and thigh lift can be shown by standing, lifting leg and 'pawing' the ground in front of you. Now lift up knee and hip higher, really reaching forward and you will reach forward several more centimetres with your 'pawing' foot and go faster.

Timed circuit

(1) Class should know that these timed runs are not races against others. They are trials against own previous best time, to be performed at a speed that makes sense to the individual.
(2) With a new class, check that they can manage the subtraction of start time from finish time. Maths problem cases can go off at 'Zero seconds', making their finish time their actual time.

Class activity

(1) Throwing for distance is difficult on a playground. Most throwing will be for accuracy. Such practising in September will contribute to their games programme.
(2) The longer overhead throw can be helped by a rocking action from rear foot to front foot with whole body coming into the throw. Aim for a good height for a catch by partner.

Group activities

(1) In a two-handed, aiming throw at a hoop, it helps to step forward with one foot into the throw, whether the throw is from the chest or from above the shoulder. Pairs can challenge others to 'best of 10 aims at the hoop'. Be sensible in longer throws and stand at a realistic distance for a high, accurate throw and easy catch.
(2) Partner holds cane loosely for safety so that it does not jar if hit. Landing softly with 'give' in the knees is important.
(3) New class will need a reminder of correct way to start a race with 'Set...go!' and how to start, stop and read the stopwatch. Runners are encouraged to 'Finish fast, right past line.'
(4) Receiving partner crouches with back to partner, right arm back with inverted V of thumb and first finger held steady to receive the baton. He or she starts running when incoming runner passes a check mark on the playground about 4 metres back.
(5) Make rules clear for fun runs. 'In quick walking, there is always one foot on the ground. Bounding means twice your normal stride. Skip all the way, not one skip then a quick run.'

Shuttle relays

Check your starting position. This is where you will finish after a run to opposite end, then a run back to starting end. Carry and receive the baton in your right hand so that you do not spear your receiver in the tummy. Stand still until you have received the baton. (Teacher judges and times the one or two races.)

LESSON PLAN • 30–50 MINUTES

WARM-UP ACTIVITIES   3–4 minutes

(1) Follow leader into good spaces as he or she shows you a mixture of running, hurdling, and jumping long and high over the lines.

(2) Keep going and remember that your take-off foot in long and high jumping and hurdling might be different to your partner's.

TIMED CIRCUIT OF 150 METRES   3–5 minutes

(1) Seven months on from last September's 150-metre timed runs, there should now be an improvement. You are older, your legs are longer, and all the gymnastic activities, dance, games and summer term athletic activities should have made you fitter.

(2) Groups will go off at 5 second intervals. Remember your starting and finishing times so that you can work out your circuit time. I will be impressed by a sensible, steady rhythm from start to finish – not a flying sprint start and a tired, slow finish.

CLASS ACTIVITY; Hurdling over canes on ground   5–8 minutes

Six sets of three canes are placed on the ground, 4 metres apart. Each group lines up behind one another, facing one set of three canes.
(1) Run to your cane and hurdle over it. Continue on to the next two and hurdle over them. Find out which is the foot you like to lead with. Stay

at the far end of the court for your return run.
(2) This time, run and hurdle, trying to lead with the same foot each time by saying 'Over, one, two, three, over'; taking three steps in between each hurdle.

GROUP ACTIVITIES; Five groups of six   16–28 minutes

(1) Hurdling, using two lines of three canes on low cones. All try to decide which is the leading leg over the hurdle, using three steps in between to make it work and repeat smoothly.
(2) Scissors high jump over low elastic 'bar' tied between high jump stands. Use a 3-step run-up, starting with the same foot that is used for jumping. Left, right, left and jump, or right, left, right and jump. Approach bar at 45 degrees with slow, bouncy run.
(3) Tennis ball throw with partner for control and distance. Each partner has 3 throws from end line down court. Partner marks best of three

throws, where the ball lands, not where it rolls to. If necessary, with long throwers, a court length limit should be imposed, and simply award 5 Stars to thrower.
(4) Three in a team, end to end relay. 1, on end line, passes baton to 2, on first line. 2 races to pass to 3, on second line. 3 races to touch end line, turns and races back to give baton to 2. 2 races to give it to 1 who races to start line. Each team member runs one third of court, twice.
(5) Bean bag put from a wide astride, side-on position with a partner marking and measuring best of three puts.

TEAMS OF THREE, THERE-AND-BACK RELAY   3–5 minutes

Each group has an 'A' and a 'B' team of three runners, well spaced on end line, first and second lines. Each races to one in front. Baton is

carried to end line where 3 turns and comes back to pass to 2 who runs to pass to 1 who ends race by sprinting across start line.

The lesson's main emphases include

(a) Recognising that these lessons, with their several, varied parts, require quick responses and excellent behaviour from all pupils to allow time for practising and improving.

(b) Measuring, comparing and improving own performances.

Equipment needed

- 18 canes
- 12 cones
- 10 batons
- 9 tennis balls
- stopwatch
- measuring tape
- marker domes for circuit and tennis ball throw
- high jump stands with elastic 'bar'

Warm-up activities

(1) Athletic activities will be interspersed with lots of running, ideally in unison.

(2) The running approach should be seen as an important part of hurdling, or long or high jumping; they should become aware of their take-off foot in all three.

Timed circuit

(1) Before they start, let them feel the inhibiting effects of tension by clenching hands. The tension passes through arms to neck, shoulders and chest, hampering performance. Then stand, swinging arms loosely, to feel the difference.

(2) Groups will go off at 5 second intervals, trying to relax and flow along at an easy, steady speed, thinking of self only. This is not a race against other people. Group one, zero seconds, go!

Class activity

(1) First of three canes will be on first line, always, for consistent hurdling. Adjust starting position of feet to ensure that first hurdle is reached and cleared with correct leading leg. This may mean reversing normal feet position at start.

(2) 'Over' is lead leg, up and down quickly. 'One, two, three' is the rapid striding between hurdles, moving to same leading leg clearing next cane.

Group activities

(1) Group uses two lines of three hurdles at same distance apart as in class activity, with first hurdle on line marking third of netball court. If they progress quickly, they can race each other over three hurdles and on to finish at opposite end of court.

(2) They should now know if they are left or right foot jumpers; and from which side they run in at 45 degrees, with three slow, careful steps, to clear low 'bar' easily, avoiding accidents.

(3) The court will be about 30–35 metres long. Any who can throw more than this are asked to hold back. 'Can you be clever and send it only as far as your partner who is standing on the end line?'

(4) Each of the three has a starting line from which they run after a stationary take-over. Each stays at line where they passed baton, to receive it on its way back, to finish at the starting line.

(5) 'Put' means the bean bag stays against the neck. Arm drives forward into put. Any backward hand movement is a throw and not allowed. Side-on body start, then a rear leg drive, upper body rotation and then the arm pushing forward from neck.

There-and-back relays

Main rule is 'Stand still until you receive baton in right hand'. A crouched start, one arm and leg forward, one back, helps you to a speedy take-off. Baton is received in inverted V of thumb in and first finger out. Two timed races with teacher calling out the results.

LESSON PLAN • 30–50 MINUTES

WARM-UP ACTIVITIES   3–4 minutes

(1) Walk to first line; jog to second line; run at three-quarter speed to end line, emphasising 'Straight ahead running'. Let feet, arms, shoulders and head keep on a straight ahead path.

(2) Turn around and repeat back to start line. Straight with no side to side twisting of body parts.

TIMED CIRCUIT OF 200 METRES   4–5 minutes

(1) Try to feel relaxed, as emphasised last month. Let all your movement be straight ahead as just practised. This month's rhythm will be slower than for last month's shorter run.

(2) Remember your starting and finishing times to work out your circuit time later. Let's have group five going first this month. Group five, zero seconds, go! Group four, five seconds, go! (etc.)

CLASS ACTIVITY; Relay baton exchange   5–8 minutes

(1) Half of the class space out along end line of court, baton in left hand. Receiving partner, stand on first line, holding right arm back, with inverted V between thumb and first finger out.
(2) Receive baton on the move, moving off when partner passes a mark of some sort on the ground 4–5 metres behind you. Go!
(3) New starter this time, practising the other way, receiving on the move in right hand. Ready, new number one, go!

GROUP ACTIVITIES; Five groups of six   15–28 minutes

(1) Relay, running change-over, with 3 pairs practising in same, whole court length area, starting and finishing on end lines of court. Receiving partner experiments with check marks as signal to go. Couples practise, then race each other, taking turns to be the starter.
(2) Overarm, bean bag throw for distance and accuracy with partners aiming to land bean bag in each other's hoop, at 15–20 metres, from a side-towards, arm-back starting position.
(3) 50-metre timed sprint around cone at 25 metres and back. There should be improvement compared with the times in September.
(4) High jump, scissors style, over low (about 45 cm) elastic 'bar' tied between high jump stands. A 'bouncy', 3-step run has same foot starting run and jumping. Nearer leg swings up and over.
(5) Throwing hoop to partner for accuracy at medium distance, about 20 metres apart. Start side-on to partner, feet wide apart, arm with hoop well back. In discus style throw, hoop is pulled around flat at shoulder height and released, straight ahead of thrower.

SIX IN A LINE RELAY   3–5 minutes

| End line   First line | X1 X2 X3 X4 X5 X6   End line |

1 starts at first line and races to touch end line, turns and races past team to touch other end line, turns and races to give baton to 2 who repeats it all. Baton is received in right hand on right side of team line and transferred to left hand for carrying and giving. Teacher at front of line calls out results and times two or three races. From a standing receipt in first race, they change to a moving receipt in races two and three.

The lesson's main emphases include

(a) Enjoyment of these varied summer-term lessons in the fresh air with their running, jumping, throwing, relays and much competition.

(b) Developing and refining basic techniques in running, relays, and throwing for accuracy and distance.

Equipment needed

- 15 batons
- 9 bean bags
- 9 hoops
- measuring tape
- stopwatch
- high jump stands and elastic 'bar'
- marker cones for circuit and 50-metre sprint

Warm-up activities

(1) Thirds of netball court are ideal for this three-part activity.
(2) Teacher observes them running towards him or her, sees and demonstrates with excellent performers who have neat, 'straight ahead' action. Then more practice to copy the good example.

Timed circuit

(1) We don't want slow marathon jogging, but we don't want high speed sprinting at start, either. Keep a sensible, steady pace and finish, recovering quickly for the rest of the lesson.
(2) Keep outside the marker cones, but don't run very wide of outside lines of netball court or you will add more distance.

Class activity

(1). End to end lines of netball court as start and finish, and middle third as a marked take-over area make this an ideal practice place. Teacher demonstrates an 'inverted V'.
(2) 'Mark on ground' can be any distinctive mark such as line, crack, different coloured patch.
(3) After several practices, they can all have races against one another, followed by demonstration by outstanding couples.

Group activities

(1) Baton receiver should say to self 'Running, running, reaching, taking' as a guide to when to prepare for take-over, after about 10 metres of running. Inverted V of right hand must be held steady as an easy target for partner responsible for transfer.
(2) Each alternates throwing/aiming three bean bags with receiving and collecting. Overarm throw means bending arm to come high over the shoulder before stretching into aim and throw.
(3) Groups need a reminder of how to start, stop and read the watch and how to start the runner they are timing. For example: 'Set…go!'
(4) Last step of this 3-step bouncy approach is a rock up from heel, ball and toes of foot further from bar. Low bar means a safe landing, completely under control.
(5) Hoop starts well back with a straight arm, fingers over and thumb under, held flat. Rear leg drives. Upper body rotates and arm is pulled with long slinging action as body finishes facing front and target.

Six in a line relay

If first race has a stationary take-over of baton by everyone, the winning time can easily be improved upon by changing to a running take-over in the second and third races, time permitting.

Such improvement, through never letting baton stop moving, demonstrates perfectly the reason for the running change we want. Teacher tries to call out finishing order.

LESSON PLAN • 30–50 MINUTES

WARM-UP ACTIVITIES   3–4 minutes

(1) Jog beside partner, trying to keep in step, exactly together. Visit all parts of the playground.
(2) Jog, one behind the other. Front person, can you remember the rhythm already done? When I call 'Change!' the following partner sprints ahead to become the new leader, jogging again.

TIMED CIRCUIT OF 200 METRES   4–5 minutes

(1) Keep outside the marker cones. Run at your own steady, sensible speed and try to keep your rhythm going to the end.
(2) Listen carefully for your start time which you will be subtracting from your finishing time. Group one, zero seconds, go! Group two, five seconds, go! (etc.)

CLASS ACTIVITY; Throwing tennis ball   5–8 minutes

(1) Stand 4–5 metres apart and throw underarm to your partner.
(2) Catcher, hold both cupped hands forward as a target for your partner to aim at. Let the hands 'give' to stop ball bouncing out.
(3) Move further apart until you need to start throwing overarm, then do not move any further apart. Stand side-on, starting with arm well back, then bending to come high over shoulder into stretch, aim, throw. (Less than court width apart for control.)
(4) How many successful throws and catches can you make out of ten?

GROUP ACTIVITIES; Five groups of six   15–28 minutes

(1) Tennis ball throw, end to end, for a measured distance – but no greater than length of court. Partner judges and measures where ball lands, and marks best of three with dome shaped cone.
(2) Partners, standing long jump across width of court, counting number of leaps to take them across. One does standing long jump from line, lands and stands still. Partner jumps next from line of jumper's toes, lands and stands still. They repeat and try to improve back to start.
(3) Hurdling down one of two lanes of three hurdles – canes on pairs of cones. Run from end line to first hurdle at first line, trying to lead with correct leg, then do 'Over, 1, 2, 3, over' taking three strides between hurdles. Pairs can race each other.
(4) Two pairs throw a large ball across middle third to clear heads and hands of pair in the middle. Use a two-handed throw from above and behind head to gain height and distance. Pairs alternate.
(5) How far can you run in 5 seconds? Partner is challenged to tell marking partner where to stand as estimate of 5 seconds run. One of markers is timekeeper and calls 'Set…go! and all sprint off. On fifth second, timekeeper shouts 'Now!' and runners check distance covered.

SHUTTLE RELAYS; 30 metres apart   3–5 minutes

    X5 X3 X1 | | X2 X4 X6

1 races to give baton to 2, then stays at back of opposite line. 2 races to give baton to 3 and stays at end of opposite line. All race stay, then race back in opposite direction to end of own starting positions. Race ends with 5 giving baton to leader 1. Right hand is used to carry and receive baton.

LESSON NOTES • 3 LESSONS DEVELOPMENT

The lesson's main emphases include

(a) Praising the class for their good quality listening and responding which is the main reason for their near-continuous action.

(b) Measuring, comparing and improving performances, always being mindful of others.

Equipment needed

- 15 tennis balls
- 5 batons
- 1 large ball
- stopwatch
- measuring tape
- 6 canes and 12 cones to make hurdles
- marker cones for throws and circuit

Warm-up activities

(1) Visit every part of our playground and 'classroom', looking for good spaces. Jogging is easy with arms and heels carried low. 'Feel' the 1, 2, 3, 4; 1, 2, 3, 4 repeating rhythm.

(2) Accelerating partner leans into more rapid striding, with greater lift of heels and knees, to become leader, before returning to easy, relaxed jogging.

Timed circuit

(1) Teacher can invite class to 'On the spot, show me how fast you intend to run this quite long circuit', to encourage sensible planning aimed at keeping going all the way.

(2) Emphasise the sense in running near the line of the circuit, not wide of it, adding to an already longish run by many metres.

Class activity

(3) The overarm throwing will start at about 12–15 metres, just inside a court's width, and none should be allowed to stand wider than a court width apart, good for accurate throwing.

Demonstrate with a good, side-on, arm bending high over shoulder action, particularly if rear leg drive and upper body rotation are seen to be helping transfer of weight into throw.

Group activities

(1) Throwers move from cross-court to length-of-court maximum for measuring their throws. Do not allow any wildly erratic throwing.

(2) Start with feet slightly apart and arms stretched above head. Bend knees and swing arms behind back. Drive up and forward with legs and swing arms into action. Land and be still to let partner start at the correct place, opposite first jumper's toes.

(3) Leading leg in hurdling goes up and down straight over hurdle. Trailing leg lifts and bends

up and out sideways, then pulls round and down to land in front to continue running forward.

(4) Teacher can adjust gap between two pairs of throwers if they are too far apart to start with, to clear opposition successfully.

(5) Estimates of distance possible in 5 seconds will be wildly over-optimistic and probably nothing like the 35–45 metres estimated. First 2 or 3 seconds will be taken up with getting into running strides from being stationary.

Shuttle relays

If halves of teams are off-set to the left of each other at their opposite ends, they will more easily pass the baton to each other, without spearing one another in the stomach.

Main rule is 'Take baton standing still, behind

your line' and it helps to 'Hold your hand forward and still, with an inverted V between thumb and first finger, for incoming runner to aim at'.

Teacher calls out race results and times the one or two races.

LESSON PLAN • 30–50 MINUTES

WARM-UP ACTIVITIES   3–4 minutes

(1) Partners, side by side, practise quick walking with bent arm action, always ensuring that one foot is on the ground.
(2) Partners stand side by side down middle of netball court. Each does a quick walk to touch nearer side line, turns and walks back to finish beside partner. After this practice, they have two competitive quick walks, with teacher calling results.

TIMED CIRCUIT OF 250 METRES   4–5 minutes

(1) Start at sensible speed, well within yourself. Choose to run or jog, or run and jog. Keep near to the outside line of the circuit to keep the distance as short as possible.
(2) Let's keep well apart as groups go off at 10 second intervals. Remember that you will be subtracting start time from finish time. Group one, zero seconds, go! Group two, ten seconds, go! (etc.)

CLASS ACTIVITY; Scissors jump over low cane   5–8 minutes

(1) Partner with cane, find a good space well away from all other jumpers. You can sit down, or kneel, one knee down, one up, as you hold the cane gently and low at about 40 cm only.
(2) Jumper, take a 3-count run in and jump from foot furthest from cane, coming in at an angle of about 45 degrees. After landing, stay on that side, turn around and come back in again, with three steps.
(3) Partner holding cane, watch your partner's action – nearer leg swings up and over 'bar', back foot does jump. After six practices, change over.

GROUP ACTIVITIES; Five groups of six   15–28 minutes

(1) Scissors jump over low (45 cm) elastic 'bar' tied between high jump stands. A slow, 3-step approach starting with the same foot used as the jumping foot. Left, right, left and jump; or right, left, right and jump.
(2) 50-metre timed sprint around a cone at 25 metres and back. Finish fast, right past time-keeper.
(3) Measured bean bag put from a line. Partner marks best of three with a dome cone. A side-on starting position with bean bag against neck. Hand and bag may only go forward from neck into push. Any hand movement back becomes a throw and is not allowed.
(4) Relay practice, down length of court, with baton exchange in middle third of netball court. Pairs practise in one direction, rest, then practise in opposite direction. Baton is received in right hand, from partner's left, on the move.
(5) Fun runs, across court and back. Encourages fun and quick reaction to 'Set…go!' by one of group, taking his or her turn: (a) quick walking; (b) sprinting; (c) skipping; (d) own invented simple run.

ROUND ONE COURT RELAY   3–5 minutes

One netball court has three teams lined up at starting places. The other court has two. All start on inside of line round court. First runner stands, ready, just outside line. On 'Go!' by teacher, 1 races once around own netball court and passes baton to 2 who has stepped out, ready to receive it in right hand, on the move, from left hand of 1. Race ends after all have run once with baton back to 1. Teacher calls out results and winner's time.

The lesson's main emphases include

(a) Experiencing the pleasure of strong partner and group 'togetherness'.

(b) Observing the conventions of fair play, honest competition and good sporting behaviour.

Equipment needed

- 15 canes
- 9 bean bags
- 5 batons
- stopwatch
- measuring tape
- marker cones for circuit and bean bag measurement

Warm-up activities

(1) The body is upright with minimal forward lean in quick walking. Arms are bent to move quickly to balance the quick steps. There must always be one foot on the ground or it becomes running, leaping or jumping.

(2) Explain race clearly. 'Walk to your nearer side line, touch it with a foot, turn and walk back to partner, finish side by side. Set...go!' The teacher calls out finishing places.

Timed circuit

(1) After the highly competitive walking it is good to remind them 'This circuit run is not a race. It is a test of how well you can organise yourself to cover the distance and still recover quickly to carry on with your lesson.'

(2) After run, teacher checks 'Can you all work out your circuit time? Did anyone go off too quickly? How do you feel?'

Class activity

(1) Cane must be held low and loosely so that it does not impede anyone. A slow careful, 3-step run-up and jump is as safe as landing during skipping.

(2) Diagonal line through cane is approach line from both sides of cane, because same side of body will be towards cane both times.

(3) Partner becomes teacher, checking angle of approach, drive from correct, further-away foot, and swing up and over by nearer leg.

Group activities

(1) The scissor jump, 3-step approach is now practised over the more familiar setting of stands and 'bar'. Good examples of slow but bouncy 3-step approach with a rock up on to heel, ball and toes of jumping foot should be demonstrated.

(2) Comparison with previously recorded 50-metre times are of interest, encouraging and, hopefully, a clear proof of improved cardiovascular health and muscular strength.

(3) A demonstration of correct, non-throwing action is an essential. From wide astride side-on start, drive forward with the rear leg; rotate upper body and shoulders; then explode into the put with hand pushing straight forward and up from neck.

(4) A good guide to covering 10 metres before even reaching back for baton is to say 'Running, running, reaching, taking'. Incoming runner should understand this planning and delay transfer.

(5) These short, good, fun competitions within own group can be developed by asking 'Can anyone plan any other simple, fun races?'

Round netball court relay

Pupils enjoy a circular relay. This is a way of arranging one without several groups starting at the same place, with those on outside running wider and further than the rest.

There should be time for a second race, with both being timed, and teacher calling out as many results as possible.

LESSON PLAN • 30–50 MINUTES

WARM-UP ACTIVITIES   3–4 minutes

(1) Can you show me that you understand the difference between jogging and running? Do about 10 seconds of each. Go!
(2) Show me jogging only, please, using those easy, small steps with your heels and arms carried low, loose, and very relaxed with no stiffness or tension. Jog, 2, 3, 4; jog, 2, 3 4; jog, 2, 3, 4.
(3) Now show me your running with its livelier lifting of heels, knees and arms, and reaching forward further with each stride. Go!

TIMED CIRCUIT OF 150 METRES   3–5 minutes

To help you with quick subtraction of start time from finishing time, we will have three runs – groups one and two; then three and four; then five by themselves. You will be taking away zero seconds if you go first, ten seconds if you go second and twenty seconds if you go third. Groups one and two, zero seconds, go! Groups three and four, ten seconds, go! Group five, twenty seconds, go!

GROUP ACTIVITIES; Five groups of six   20–35 minutes

(1) Timed 50-metre sprint around a cone at 25 metres. Each team member has a turn at being starter and timekeeper; then telling runner their time; then having own time recorded.
(2) Standing long jump from a side line. Measurement is by reference to the 2-metre sticks placed parallel to the line of jump.
Each takes turn at jumping from standing position; being told the distance by team mate at side of metre sticks; waiting to tell next jumper their distance. Each one's best jump is added together for recording.
(3) Bean bag put from side line, each having 4 puts, the best of which is marked and measured by partner. Any backward hand movement is a throw and not allowed.
(4) Non-scoring run over three hurdles – canes on pairs of cones – trying to make three running strides in between hurdles. Over; 1, 2, 3, over. On the way back to start of hurdles, they can practise a scaled-down, hop, step and jump, trying to feel and hear the equal rhythm of the three parts – each just over one metre in distance – which will not jar legs.
(5) Throwing a large ball, starting with both arms above and behind head, and one foot in front of the other for balance and power. Partner marks and measures the best of three attempts.

TEAM SHUTTLE RELAYS; Width of court   4–6 minutes

X5 X3 X1 | Side line of court   Side line of court | X2 X4 X6

1 races to give baton to 2, right hand to right hand, then goes to end of line behind 6. 2 races to give baton to 3, and stays at back of line, behind 5. All race one way, then back the other to starting places. Race ends with 1 receiving baton from 5.

Team Number _____

First place in activity gains five points for a team. Fifth place gains one point.

Event	Individual Results						Combined Result	Place 1st–5th	Points 5–1
	1	2	3	4	5	6			
150 m									
50 m									
Standing long jump									
Bean bag put									
Large ball throw									
Shuttle relay									
								Total Points Position in Class	

49

LESSON PLAN • 30–50 MINUTES

WARM-UP ACTIVITIES   3–4 minutes

(1) Show me your best running, visiting all parts of this court. Is your running silent with a good lift of heels and knees?
(2) Half running, now, half watching. Watchers, tell me whose running you like, and why.
(3) Thank you for your helpful comments. Now, let's watch the other half. Observers will then tell me who you particularly liked and why. Go! (More comments, thanks, then all have a last practice to try to improve, remembering the good points mentioned.)

TIMED CIRCUIT OF 150 METRES   3–5 minutes

(1) Your medium speed, steady running just practised is about right for the timed circuit which is not a race. Steady all the way.
(2) Groups one, two and three will be timed first, then groups four and five will go. Remember to subtract starting time from finishing time. Group one, zero seconds, go! Group two, five seconds, Go! (etc.)

CLASS ACTIVITY; Throwing large ball   5–8 minutes

(1) Three players make a triangle, 3 metres apart. Chest-pass around triangle with fingers well spread.
(2) A bigger triangle, 5 metres apart. Ball starts beside shoulder and arms are pushed towards partner. Relax arms on catching.

GROUP ACTIVITIES; Five groups of six   16–28 minutes

(1) Two trios in a 4 metre-sided triangle. 1 throws large ball to 2, runs to 2's position, and back to own place. 2 passes to 3, runs to 3's place, then back to own place. 3 throws to 1, and so it continues, passing, following and running back to own place.
(2) Scissors jump over low (45 cm) elastic 'bar' tied between high jump stands. By now, all should know from which side to approach at 45-degree angle. Three strides only are taken to prevent over-speeding and slipping at take-off and on landing.
(3) 50-metre timed sprint around a cone at 25 metres. They will compare time, back in class, with the many taken over two years. Group members take turns at starting and timekeeping; telling the runner the time; then waiting to be timed, individually.
(4) Throwing hoop for accuracy and medium distance across width of netball court. Start, side-on to partner, with hoop held well back and almost touching ground. Flat hoop is pulled on semi-circle straight past shoulder, then released in front of head.
(5) Partner fun races across width of court: (a) Three-legged race, side by side, hands behind back, left hand in left, right hand in right; (b) quick walking, one to line and back, then partner to line and back; (c) sprinting, there and back; (d) any of own creation.

SHUTTLE RELAYS; 30 metres apart   3–5 minutes

    X5 X3 X1 | | X2 X4 X6
1 races to pass baton to 2, and stays at back of 2's line. 2 races to pass baton to 3 and stays at back of 3's line. All run and stay, there and back, to finish in starting places.

The lesson's main emphases include

(a) Re-establishing good traditions and habits of safe, sensible practice, wholehearted participation and a ready response to instructions.

(b) Refining basic techniques in running, jumping and throwing.

Equipment needed

- 10 large balls
- 5 batons
- 3 hoops
- stopwatch
- marker cones for circuit
- high jump stands and elastic 'bar'

Warm-up activities

(1) In good running, there is an impression of lightness and lift in heels, knees, head and shoulders.
(2) Observers like running that is quiet, well spaced apart from others, and constantly changing direction to visit all parts.
(3) Half watching, half working often results in the teacher having an excellent performer newly discovered by a pupil observer.

Timed circuit

(1) 'Medium speed' is between brisk and very brisk for this shortish distance, but less than full speed sprinting.
(2) Greater interest in results is helped by teacher calling 'Eighteen and nineteen and twenty and twenty one' as they finish, with the 'and' meaning 0.5 seconds, to give a more accurate time, as they subtract starting time from finishing time.

Class activity

(1) The athletic activity throwing of large ball is also appropriate for start of winter games programme with its netball, basketball and other small-sided games.

(2) Hands starting by shoulders can give a longer, more vigorous throw, much used in netball. Partner must go out to meet ball and let hands and arms 'give' on receiving it.

Group activities

(1) This 'Throw, follow pass to catcher, run back' practice keeps all three on their toes to be back before the ball comes to them a second time. Trios can compete to 'Make twelve passes first.'
(2) There will be no slipping at take-off, or stumbling on landing if jumpers take only a slow, 3-step run up before take-off. The slow run up can be bouncy enough to produce a lively jump and a good, safe and controlled landing.
(3) A September reminder is needed to explain how to start, stop and read the stopwatch, and how to start each individual runner so that times are consistent and reliable, from month to month.
(4) Hoop throw across width of netball court is a popular activity, done like a discus throw. Because of limited space, the throw is for accuracy and distance limited to court width only. A pulling, whirling arm action starts directly behind and comes around to side at shoulder height.
(5) In the three-legged, side-by-side race, inside feet lift on 'Set!', on 'Go!' they both step down on inside foot and run, balanced, two inner, then two outer feet. They can be challenged 'Can you invent any other good fun partner races?'

Shuttle relays

Ideally, halves of teams face each other slightly off-set to left. Baton is then carried and passed easily from right hand to right hand with no possibility of spearing the recipient (as could happen if on same line, using different hands).

Year 5 • April • Playground Lesson 2

LESSON PLAN • 30–50 MINUTES

WARM-UP ACTIVITIES   3–4 minutes

(1) Follow your leader, 3 metres apart. Walk to first line; jog to second line; run at three-quarter speed across end line, emphasising good heel and knee lift to reach well forward.

(2) Turn around with a new leader to walk, jog, run; this time thinking 'Straight ahead' action with feet, arms, shoulders travelling straight, with no twisting, side to side movements. (Repeat both)

TIMED CIRCUIT OF 150 METRES   4–5 minutes

(1) Run this medium distance at the three-quarter speed you have just practised. Too often, too many of you go off at full speed.
(2) Let's have groups five, four and three going first and being timed, then groups two and one.

Remember to subtract start time from finish time for your circuit time. Group five, zero seconds, go! Group four, five seconds, go! Group three, ten seconds, go!

CLASS ACTIVITY; Hop, step and jump   5–8 minutes

(1) Jog easily up to the long side line of the netball court and find out which is your hopping foot. It will only be a small hop that leaves you with lots of forward speed to spare.
(2) As you go back to the starting place, try a walk into a hop and then a step. That is, one foot

to the same foot to the opposite foot.
(3) Easy run up to line again, and try a hop and a bounding step.
(4) Try a hop, step and jump whose rhythm has roughly equal parts – not a huge hop, a tiny step and a poor little jump.

GROUP ACTIVITIES; Five groups of six   15–28 minutes

(1) Triple jump after easy run up to side line. Aim for a hop of about 1 metre, then a step and a jump of about the same length. These distances will not hurt your feet and ankles.
(2) Tennis ball throw with a partner marking where the ball lands, always to be no longer than the length of a netball court. Throw from a side-on start, with feet wide apart and arm well back. Arm bends high over shoulder, then stretches into aim and throw.
(3) Hurdling over three sets of canes on cones in two lanes, with first hurdle on first line. Try to run up to lead with correct leg over first hurdle, then say to self 'Over, 1, 2 , 3, over' with three strides in

between hurdles, and same leg always leading.
(4) Scissors jump at 45 degrees to elastic 'bar' tied between high jump stands at a low height, about 45 cm. Start three strides from the bar, starting on the same foot that becomes the take-off foot. Use a slow, bouncy approach for a good, safe take-off and soft landing.
(5) Relay baton exchange with partner receiving baton within middle third of netball court, between first and second lines. First runner carries in left hand. Partner, moving forward, receives it in right hand's inverted V of thumb and first finger. Plan a take-over at 10–12 metres.

LONG LINE, END TO END RELAY   3–5 minutes

Line 1 | X1 X2 X3 X4 X5 X6 | Line 2
1 races to touch Line 1, races past team to touch line 2 and runs back to give baton to 2 who

repeats it all. 1 goes to end of line behind 6. Race ends with baton back to 1.

LESSON NOTES • 3 LESSONS DEVELOPMENT

The lesson's main emphases include

(a) Enjoying the variety in each of the lessons – running, relays, hurdling, jumping, throwing.
(b) Making simple judgements about own and others' performances and using this information to improve the quality of own performance.

Equipment needed

- 6 canes on 12 cones to make hurdles
- 5 batons
- 3 tennis balls
- high jump stands and elastic 'bar'
- measuring tape
- marker cones for circuit and throws

Warm-up activities

(1) Pairs try to mirror each other, step for step, feeling improved stride length that comes from emphasis on lifting knees and heels.
(2) Now straightness is being mirrored, particularly in the way that arms and feet move straight forward and back, down line of run.

Timed circuit

(1) 'Three quarter speed' running means leaving something in reserve, not going at full speed sprinting. We still want the good quality features as practised in warm-up, because they are energy-efficient, more productive and less tiring.
(2) Teacher emphasises 'Do not cut corners. Run around the marker cones, keeping as close to the line of the run as possible to prevent adding lots of extra metres. Relax and be steady.'

Class activity

(1) Explain 'A hop is when you spring from and land on the same foot'. Right to right or left to left.
(2) Try for a hop and a step of roughly equal parts. Often pupils do a long hop, leaving no forward momentum for a good step.
(3) Feel the stepping leg reaching up and ahead for a good step.
(4) Demonstrate with good performers showing 'One...and two...and three. Into hop; into bounding step; into a vigorous jump.'

Group activities

(1) The scaled-down version of triple jump prevents painful impact on knees and ankles, landing on the playground, and makes it easier to practise the three equal parts.
(2) Each thrower has three throws with long throwers restrained to stay within the length of the court if necessary. Distances can be read from a tape along the side line.
(3) Leading leg goes straight up and down over hurdle to start running again. Trailing leg has to lift up and out to side before pulling round and down, to avoid it hitting top of hurdle.
(4) Jumpers can run in with their three slow, springy, controlled steps from both sides of bar. The 45 degrees approach line applies to both sides of bar. Jump; land; turn and step back to 3-step distance; run in and jump over bar set low to make landing on playground safe.
(5) Both runners need to know that the change-over is not wanted or expected until about 10–12 metres of running through take-over area. Receiver can judge this by calling to himself and partner 'Running; running; reaching; taking' which needs about 10 metres.

Long line, end to end, relay

Baton change-over can take place within the middle third lines as practised, from runner's left hand to receiver's right hand. Teacher tries to call out all results and times winning team. Time permitting, run a second race.

LESSON PLAN • 30–50 MINUTES

WARM-UP ACTIVITIES   3–4 minutes

(1) In lines of sixes, can you quick walk behind a leader and keep a metre between you? End person jogs to front as new leader. Next end person then jogs to front.
(2) Lines now jog behind leader and end person has to sprint past team to front.
(3) Let's have an inter-group race, doing the two activities just practised, and finish, standing still behind original leader.

TIMED CIRCUIT OF 200 METRES   4–5 minutes

(1) May I remind you that this is not a race? It is a time trial to see how well you judge your running rhythm for this distance.
(2) After your run I will ask 'Have you worked out your time? Was your rhythm just right or too fast? Did you recover quickly?'

CLASS ACTIVITY; Relay baton exchange   5–8 minutes

(1) 1, baton in left hand, on end line, runs fast to give baton to 2, within the take-over area, in the middle third of court. 2 receives it in right hand at 10–12 metres point. Ready…go!
(2) 2 starts run. Both plan change-over at about 10–12 metres after partner starts running.
(3) Practise both ways again. Receiver, see if you can find a helpful check mark on the ground.
(4) Now, let's have two races, all against all, one in each direction.

GROUP ACTIVITIES; Five groups of six   15–28 minutes

(1) Partners, relay take-over practice, still within centre third of court, running at speed, to receive baton at the planned spot. Then couples race couples, starting and finishing on end lines.
(2) Throwing hoop for distance down length of court. Thrower stands side-on to line of throw, feet astride, arm and hoop well back. Action is a pull with straight arm at shoulder height to a point in front of head for aim and release. Hoop is kept flat.
(3) 50-metre timed sprint, around a marker at 25 metres and back. Each takes turn at starting/ timekeeping; telling runner his or her time, then being timed, individually. Finish fast!
(4) Putting the bean bag for distance across court with partner marking the best of three puts. Bean bag must start against neck with elbow high behind it. A put is a movement forward from neck. Any movement back from neck is a throw and not allowed.
(5) Partners standing long jump across width of court. 1 does a standing long jump and stands still. 2 does next jump from where 1 landed. They continue jumping alternately to see how many leaps they need to cross to other side – competing with own previous best and others.

THREES, THERE-AND-BACK RELAY   3–5 minutes

X1 │	X2 │	X3 │	│ End
X4 │	X5 │	X6 │	│ line

Each group has two trios with each member at a line. 1 and 4 race to give baton to 2 and 5 who race to give baton to 3 and 6 who race to end line, turn and repeat the process back to start line with 1 and 4. They take baton, standing, in this small area.

The lesson's main emphases include

(a) Praising pupils for responding immediately and moving from activity to activity quickly, to enable all parts of the lesson to be successfully achieved.

(b) Measuring, comparing and improving own performances.

Equipment needed

- 15 batons
- 9 bean bags
- 3 hoops
- stopwatch
- measuring tape
- marker cones for throws and marking circuit

Warm-up activities

(1) A good leader gives the team good space to work in, and keeps a steady rhythm. A jog is quick enough for overtaking quick walking. Only one person at a time overtakes.

(2) Sprinting is needed to overtake five other joggers.

(3) In the races, group against group, emphasise 'No end person may overtake until previous overtaker has reached front.'

Timed circuit

(1) You are running to try for a good personal time. You are not concerned with others. Better technique is one way to improve your own result. Relax hands, arms and legs to remove all inhibiting tension. Lift heels and knees to help to increase your stride length, with each step taking you nearer the end.

(2) I will call '33 and 34 and 35 and…' as you finish, with the 'and' meaning 0.5 seconds, to give you a more accurate time.

Class activity

(1) Half of class line up on one end line. Partners line up at first line, one third way down court, to receive baton.

(2) Most primary pupils take baton far too early, too slowly.

(3) 'Check mark' on ground can be any distinctive mark, line, darker or lighter area on surface of playground.

(4) Well practised, they need a race to try it out properly.

Group activities

(1) Two- or three-partner relay practices, checking on when to start running and when to start receiving, are followed by races.

(2) Hoop throwers are limited to a narrow, court width sector, for hoop to land in. Tape can be along a side line for easy reading.

(3) Suggest a crouch start with one foot and arm forward, one back, to assist early rapid striding in the sprint. We want an explosive response to 'Go!' and a fast finish with no early slowing down.

(4) Putter aims high at about 60 degrees for release of bean bag, after a rear leg drive forward, an upper body rotation and the push straight forward from neck.

(5) In a standing long jump, feet start slightly apart. Arms swing up high, then knees bend and arms swing down behind. Legs drive up and forward accompanied by strong arm swing forward. Legs bend to land as far forward as possible.

Threes, there-and-back relay

This is easily organised with lines spaced equally apart on netball court. Because the distance between lines is short, we take baton standing still. After giving baton, each stands waiting to have the baton returned on the line where they made earlier change-over.

LESSON PLAN • 30–50 MINUTES

WARM-UP ACTIVITIES   3–4 minutes

(1) Groups start along end line. Walk to first line. Jog to second line. Sprint to other end line, counting number of strides needed.
(2) Turn around to repeat it all the way back, walking, jogging, sprinting. See if you need fewer strides to cross the final third. If your striding speed is the same, you must be running faster.

TIMED CIRCUIT OF 250 METRES   4–5 minutes

(1) This is your own timed run, not a race against others. Show me that you can do this distance sensibly and calmly and finish up getting your breath back quickly without being shattered.
(2) Running wide, away from line of circuit, will add many metres to your already longish distance. Run beside the line.

CLASS ACTIVITY; Tennis ball throw   5–8 minutes

(1) We have always thrown from a standing position. Today we will add a couple of steps to give you more power. All stand with feet together, side-on to the line of throw, arm back. Step rear foot across front foot. Long step to side with other foot, still side-on, leaning well back over rear foot. Practise without a ball.
(2) At court width apart only, carefully practise with a ball, trying those two steps, moving forward in the side-on position. Forward arm is up to balance the lean back of your upper body. Arm bends high to come over shoulder, then stretches into careful throw.

GROUP ACTIVITIES; Five groups of six   15–28 minutes

(1) Stepping into tennis ball throw for greater power. Even more power can be added by jumping from one foot into the 'side-on, step and throw' jump from foot opposite to throwing arm.
(2) Hurdling over three sets of hurdles – canes on pairs of cones. Adjust starting position of feet to ensure you reach the first hurdle with the correct leading leg going over bar first.
(3) Scissors high jumping over elastic 'bar' tied between high jump stands. Use a slow, careful, controlled 3- or 5-step approach, starting the run-up with same foot that you jump with. Approach bar at angle of 45 degrees, with nearer leg swinging up and over.
(4) Throwing large ball with 2-step approach. Start with ball above and behind head with arms straight. Take one step forward with upper body leaning back. Take a second step forward and throw with the feeling of weight coming into vigorous throw.
(5) 75-metre timed sprint, three trips around a cone at 25 metres. Starter/timekeeper is at opposite end to the starters.

ROUND AND ROUND CIRCUIT, ONE MINUTE RELAY   3–5 minutes

One netball court has three teams lined up at starting places, well apart on inside of court. Other netball court has two teams. First runners stand on 'track', just outside line. On 'Go!' 1 races once around their own court and passes baton to 2 who has stepped out, ready to receive it in the right hand from 1's left hand. Teams continue for one minute of running and baton passing until teacher calls 'Stop!' then checks on the circuits and part circuits travelled by each team.

LESSON NOTES • 3 LESSONS DEVELOPMENT

The lesson's main emphases include

(a) Vigorous participation in these very physical, fresh-air lessons to develop flexibility, strength, and stamina.

(b) Learning to pace themselves in challenges.

Equipment needed

- 15 tennis balls
- 6 canes on 12 cones to make hurdles
- 3 large balls
- high jump stands and elastic 'bar'
- measuring tape for throws
- stop watch

Warm-up activities

(1) Counting your sprint strides is done by counting left or right foot strides, depending on which foot hits the line, and doubling the score.

(2) Proof that raising knee and hip adds to distance is shown by standing on one leg, raising other leg a little way and seeing how far ahead you can 'paw' the ground. Now do same thing after a good lift of knee and thigh before reaching forward to 'paw' ground again. Distance reached will be several centimetres greater.

Timed circuit

(1) We want this run to be proof of improved fitness by improved times during the month, and by ability to recover and feel ready to continue working.

(2) Another way to keep times down is to run near line, relax and lift knees and heels to reach well forward into good strides.

Class activity

(1) If unrestrained, they will take many running steps as a preparation for throwing, doing more running than throwing. Taking two steps, only, as explained, will help them do as well, and in a more controlled way.

(2) As in all throwing, there is: (a) the rear leg drive forward; (b) the upper body rotation; (c) the pulling action into the throw. In this they bend the arm high over one shoulder to stretch it into the throw and follow-through. Use a limited throw across court.

Group activities

(1) The jump into side-on, step, step and throw needs to be practised, coordinating the turn of body, the lean back with arm going behind, and then using leg, body and arm in that order to transfer weight into throw and follow-through.

(2) A run from end line to hurdle on first line of court gives a consistent run-in so they start in a position to ensure that the correct leg leads over first hurdle every time. Three steps in between as they think 'Over, 1, 2, 3, over'.

(3) If they choose a 5-step approach it must be slow and bouncy and completely under control to give a safe, easy landing after clearing the low (45 cm) 'bar'. This landing should be no more fraught than landing from a run and jump, such as one does in netball.

(4) Once again, they have to be restrained from a long, running throw and made to use the 2-step approach with the strong backward bend and a forceful, long arm throw.

(5) They will only have one timed run each for maximum effort.

Round and round circuit, one minute relay

Each will be running about 35 metres only as their share of 'once round', so they can sprint hard all the way, and probably the team will do 3-4 circuits, plus part of a circuit. (i.e. plus ends and sides).

LESSON PLAN • 30–50 MINUTES

WARM-UP ACTIVITIES   3–4 minutes

(1) Jog, side by side, with a partner, with one of you recalling the rhythm you used when you ran the previous lesson's 250-metre timed jog / run. I will call out 'Walk!' after 15 seconds. Go!
(2) Now the other partner tries to recall a sensible 250-metre circuit rhythm for both to follow.

Once again, I will call out 'Walk!' after 15 seconds. Go!
(3) Each have another practice at your estimated jog or run speed. When I call 'Change!' the new leader goes straight into his or her circuit rhythm, steady speed.

TIMED CIRCUIT OF 250 METRES   4–5 minutes

rhythm, steady speed.
(1) I hope that you are now able to feel and set a good steady rhythm that you can keep up without becoming shattered. If in doubt, slow down.

Run near the line – if you go wide, you run more than 250 metres.
(2) Let's have group five going off first this month. Listen for and remember your start and

CLASS ACTIVITY; Throwing a hoop   5–8 minutes

finish times. Group five, zero seconds, go! (etc.)
(1) 1s, stand astride the throwing line with hoop well back in straight arm. Grip with fingers over, thumb under, holding hoop horizontal, not pointing up.
(2) Without letting go, practise the backward and

forward rotation of straight arm, sideways pulling the hoop at shoulder height from behind you to a point in front of head and back again.
(3) Now, carefully and slowly, try the whole movement, letting go to land it by your partner, 12–15 metres away, flying flat.

GROUP ACTIVITIES; Five groups of six   15–28 minutes

(1) Throwing hoop for accuracy and medium distance across court. As before, practise the forward and backward swings without releasing it, feeling the rear leg drive, upper body rotation, and then the pull into aim and release to make it fly horizontally.
(2) Pairs race over three hurdles after run-in to first line hurdle, using three steps between hurdles – over, 1, 2, 3, over – with same leading leg every time. Pairs then race to end line of court.

(3) Measured tennis ball throw after a 2-step approach to throwing line. Partner marks and measures best of three throws.
(4) Relay baton exchange in middle third of netball court. Partners race other couples to end line after running take-over. Rest, then race the other way. Both plan take-over at 10-12 metres.
(5) Scaled-down, easy hop, step and jump, trying to make each part equal, just over a metre, so that there is no jarring of ankles. Use a short run up to the line and correct take-off foot.

ROUND THE CIRCUIT (ONE NETBALL COURT) RELAYS   3–5 minutes

One netball court has three teams, the other has two lined up at starting places, well apart on inside of line round court. 1 stands on 'track', just outside the line. On teacher's 'Go!' 1 races once

around own court and passes baton to 2 who has stepped out, ready to receive it in right hand from 1's left hand. All race around circuit and race ends with baton back in 1's hand. Teacher tries to call out winner from five teams taking

The lesson's main emphases include

part and as many results as possible.

(a) End of year praise for pupils' co-operation, enabling the lessons to be successfully carried out and progressed.

(b) Refining and extending skills and performing them with accuracy and consistency.

Equipment needed

- 15 hoops
- 5 batons
- 9 tennis balls
- measuring tape
- 3 large balls
- stopwatch

Warm-up activities

- marker cones

(1) After planning and performing many timed circuits they should be able to estimate and perform at a sensible speed.

(2) Going too fast is the main fault. Shadowing partner can slow them down to a speed that can be maintained continuously.

(3) Their well practised, estimated circuit speed should now be reproducible in the actual circuit run.

Timed circuit

(1) For a few seconds they can be asked to run on the spot at what they estimate is an appropriate speed. The teacher can deter any wildly over-speed running and advise generally.

(2) 1s usually go off first, with least time to recover from warm-up. Here, they are going off last for a change.

Class activity

(1) The teacher checks side-on, starting positions of throwers and their grip on the hoop.

(2) Pull forward and back is same as wind up by a discus thrower, feeling the weight transfer forward and back, ready for throw.

(3) Aiming at 60 degrees gives a good flight, keeping it flat like a discus. Practice is then

Group activities

repeated for partner.

(1) Short hoop throw for control and accuracy, until the correct action is learned. Then challenge them to throw it across width of court to land flat and in front of partner.

(2) Previous month's adjustment of feet starting positions is recalled as way to ensure correct leg leads over first hurdle. The leading leg goes up and down straight over. Trailing leg lifts up and around to one side to avoid bumping into hurdle.

(3) Use a 2-step approach as the preparation for the turn to side-on throw. Make court length the maximum throw allowed to prevent wildly inaccurate throwing and balls becoming lost.

(4) Baton receiver does not offer hand until well into the running action at 10–12 metres when partner is expecting take-over to take place. Most primary pupils anxiously take baton too early.

(5) Short run up for triple jump aims to bring you to line with hopping foot ready to take off. Marker cones, about 1 metre apart, guide them to short, safe, non-jarring leaps, and a good rhythm.

Round the netball court circuits

These, like round the track races on a field, are very popular and the relay part of a lesson must never be missed out. This is a very fair version because no-one is running wide at a disadvantage. There should be time for two races and the teacher will try to call out as many results as possible and time both sets of winners. Baton exchange should be becoming well co-ordinated at speed.

LESSON PLAN • 30–50 MINUTES

WARM-UP ACTIVITIES   3–4 minutes

(1) Side by side with your partner, can you keep together at the same, easy jogging speed? In jogging, arms and heels are low and your short strides keep a nice, easy, repetitive rhythm: 1, 2, 3, 4.

(2) Change to walking, side by side now. When you are ready, change to relaxed, half speed running with more of a lift of knees and heels than in the jogging. Also, stride out in a more lively way.
(3) Finally, see how well you keep together in walking, then jogging, then half speed running,

TIMED CIRCUIT OF 200 METRES   4–5 minutes

Start at a sensible running speed and you will be able to finish at an equally sensible pace. If you start off too quickly you will finish up walking and weary, gaining a poor time for your team score. Groups will go off at 5 second intervals.

GROUP ACTIVITIES; Five groups of six   20–35 minutes

(1) Timed 60-metre sprint around a cone at 30 metres. Each team member is timed individually by another team member. Runners are encouraged to 'finish fast with no slowing down at the line'.
(2) Throwing the hoop with a partner judging, marking and measuring your best of three throws across the court. Straight arm pulls hoop around from back to front at shoulder height to release just in front of the head, trying to make it fly flat to land and settle, not land upright and roll away.
(3) Trios, three standing long jumps each. 1 starts behind line, does a standing broad jump, lands and does a second and third jump. 2 stands beside 1's 'line of toes' landing place after third jump, does team's second set of three jumps and

stands still. 3 springs off from 2's final landing place. Trio result is then measured and marked as a challenge to other groups.
(4) Throwing a tennis ball for accuracy. Thrower, from behind an end line, aims to throw ball to land in the furthest third of netball court. Three careful, controlled throws are attempted, using three balls. Then fielding partner steps back to own end line to become the aiming partner. Each records best of three throws.
(5) Non-scoring hurdling over four canes on pairs of cones, trying to take off with correct leading leg, and to take three rapid strides in between hurdles. As they walk back for another practice, they can try a scaled-down, easy hop, step and jump.

TEAM SHUTTLE RELAYS; Width of court   3–6 minutes

X5 X3 X1 | Side line of court   Side line of court | X2 X4 X6

1 races to give baton to 2 – right hand to right hand – and stays at end of line. 2 races to give baton to 3 and stays at end of that line. Each races one way, stays, and later races back to own side and stays. Race ends with 1 receiving baton in own place again.
Teacher calls out results and times winning team.

Year 5 • Playground Team Competition • Score card to be carried around

Team Number _____

First place in activity gains five points for a team. Fifth place gains one point.

Event	Individual Results 1 2 3 4 5 6	Combined Result	Place 1st–5th	Points 5–1
200 m				
60 m				
Throwing hoop				
Standing long jump				
Tennis ball aiming				
Shuttle relay				
			Total Points Position in Class	

LESSON PLAN • 30–50 MINUTES

WARM-UP ACTIVITIES   3–4 minutes

(1) Run and jump high and run and jump long over the many lines on the playground. Can you show me which is your take-off foot in both kinds of jump? It's not always the same one.

(2) Now change to best running, showing me your straight-ahead running action with feet, arms, head and shoulders all travelling in a straight line with no side to side twisting as you go.

TIMED CIRCUIT OF 100 METRES   3–5 minutes

(1) Do not sprint around this distance at full speed, but do not pretend it is a marathon, either. Judge a sensible, three quarter speed, steady, relaxed rhythm that you can do all the way.

(2) Groups one to three will go off first and be timed. Then groups four and five. 'Group one, ready.'

GROUP ACTIVITIES; Throwing large ball   5–8 minutes

(1) Trios, in a triangle formation, practise 'Pass and follow'. 1 passes to 2 and runs the 5 metres to 2's place. 2 passes to 3 and runs to 3's place. 3 runs carrying ball to what was 1's place, and the practice starts again.

(2) Trios compete to 'make six sets of complete triangle runs'.

GROUP ACTIVITIES; Five groups of six   16–28 minutes

(1) Trios, 7–10 metres apart, throw large ball around their triangle formation. Ball starts above and behind head in both hands. Two steps forward are allowed to add to forward momentum and distance, always trying to give an easy catch high to partner.

(2) 50-metre timed sprint around a cone at 25 metres. A new school year reminder is given on how to start, stop and read stopwatch. Each is started/timed by another member of the group.

(3) Standing high jump over low cane held by partner, from arm's length facing cane, or side-on standing near. Six each, then revise 3-step approach and scissors jump over equally low cane. Partner checks nearer foot swings up, fur-ther foot takes off.

(4) Bean bag putting with a partner, using width of netball court. One bag is used from side to side. Putter stands side-on to line of put with bag against neck, elbow high behind. Forward arm is bent and high as balance; explosive push of arm forward from neck and cocked wrist snapping forward at the very end.

(5) Shuttle relay practices, two teams of three across width of court. Baton starts at front of line which has two runners. 1 runs to pass to 2 at opposite side and stays at back of line. 2 runs to give baton to 3 and stays at back of line. 3 races to give baton to 1, and so on until all are back to starting places.

SHUTTLE RELAYS; Court width (as above)   3–5 minutes

```
    X5  X3  X1 |              | X2  X4  X6
```
1 races to give baton to 2 and stays at end of line. Each has two runs, across and back, to finish in original starting place with baton back to 1. Teacher calls out results of this and the second race.

LESSON NOTES • 3 LESSONS DEVELOPMENT

The lesson's main emphases include

(a) Re-establishing good habits of listening, responding, and wholehearted participation by this age group with its enormous potential for high quality physical education performances.
(b) Developing and refining the basic actions of running and relays, jumping and throwing.

Equipment needed

- 10 large balls
- 5 batons
- 3 canes
- 3 bean bags
- marker cones for timed sprint and timed circuit
- stopwatch

Warm-up activities

(1) In high jumping the approach to line is at an angle. In long jumping the approach is straight at the line. Safe, sensible, scaled-down jumping does not jar ankles and knees.

(2) A demonstration of neat, 'straight ahead' action, which is not typical, will give the class a picture to remember and copy.

Timed circuit

(1) The different abilities will produce a wide variety of examples of 'sensible running you can do all the way'.

(2) The teacher can encourage 'your best straight ahead running', not wasting effort by zig-zagging instead of going forward.

Class activity

(1) This practice is a combination of throwing and speed running. Dome shaped cones can mark triangles.

(2) Style of passing can be relevant to the netball, rugby or basketball going on in games lessons.

Group activities

(1) Two steps forward into the throwing position with one foot forward and one back, and the long overhead pull combine to produce a throw that can be long and accurate. Groups can compete – 'How many 10-metre throws with a good catch can you make?'
(2) Runners start in a crouched, sprint start position, one foot and opposite arm forward, weight inclined forward ready. They are told to 'Finish fast!' and not slow down before the end line.
(3) The 'bar' is held loosely and low in jumping by partner so that it does not impede the jumper if he or she bumps into it. With a sensible 'give' of knees on landing from such low heights, there will be no painful jarring.
(4) In the side-on, feet wide astride, starting position, they have two or three preparatory rocks forward and back, as shot putters do, before their eventual upper body turn and explosive arm and wrist extension forward into put. The bean bag must never come backwards away from the neck – this is throwing and not allowed.
(5) In shuttle relays, carry and receive baton with right hand so that you are not spearing the receiver's tummy which can happen if you use different hands. They must be stationary for change-over at line.

Team shuttle relays

While group activities are the most important part of the lesson, the relays are the most exciting and should never be missed out. Halves of teams should be slightly off-set to left of each other, so that they do not spear each other with baton, running on same line.

The teacher, at start/finish line, calls out all the results and times the winners to give all groups a time to beat in the second race.

LESSON PLAN • 30–50 MINUTES

WARM-UP ACTIVITIES   3–4 minutes

(1) Jog to first line. Walk to second line. Jog to end line. Turn around and repeat back to starting line.

(2) This time jog to first line again, then try to do your 150-metre circuit speed to the end line. Turn around and repeat back.

TIMED CIRCUIT OF 150 METRES   3–5 minutes

(1) Run in such a sensible way that you can finish feeling fit to do the rest of the lesson. Relax, stride out well, don't cut corners!
(2) Keep near to the line around the court. Wide running adds many metres to your circuit. Remember to subtract start from finish times. 'Group one, zero seconds, go! Group two, five seconds, go!' (etc.)

CLASS ACTIVITY; Scaled down long jump   5–8 minutes

(1) This is a safe, careful practice of long jump after a short run. Stand, feet together on side line, with back to centre of court. Run away from the line, build up to half speed for what would be your long jump take-off. Mark the spot where speed is right.
(2) Stand with feet together at this mark. Run to the line at half speed and see if you hit line with your take-off foot for a very careful long jump, landing with feet together.
(3) Practise carefully from your mark, landing well controlled each time, after feeling the correct leading leg reach well forward.

GROUP ACTIVITIES; Five groups of six   16–28 minutes

(1) Scaled down long jumping. Partner watches your restrained run and jump to see how near your take-off foot was to the line from your marked start about 10 metres back only. Look for the front leg reaching forward and rear leg catching up for the landing.
(2) Tennis ball throw after 2-step approach. Side on, step right foot across left, taking arm back. Left foot steps wide to side. Rear leg drives forward, upper body rotates to front, and throwing arm bends to come high over shoulder into stretch, aim, throw.
(3) Hurdling over four sets of canes on pairs of cones, first at first line. Start at end line, lead with correct leg over first hurdle with three steps in between 'over, 1, 2, 3, over'. Walk back on leading leg side of hurdles, lifting trailing leg up to side, around and down.
(4) Throwing hoop for partner at 15–20 metres. Partner watches for and coaches: (a) wide, side-on stance, hoop held just under horizontal, well back in straight arm, fingers over, thumb under. (b) two or three discus style forward and backward, preparatory rotations with arm at shoulder level. (c) throw, preceded by rear leg drive, rotation of upper body, and straight arm pulling action.
(5) 60-metre timed sprint around a marker cone at 30 metres. Each team member takes turn at starting/timekeeping; telling runner the time, then running own timed sprint. 'Finish fast!'

PARTNERS, SIDE LINES TOUCH RELAYS   3–5 minutes

Partners stand, side by side, down centre of netball court. On 'Go!', 1 races to touch nearer side line, turns, races back to touch hand of partner who does same to own nearer side line. Teacher calls out results as pairs finish together. One or more races should be contested. Speed can be improved by second runner using a crouched, sprint start position for explosive start.

The lesson's main emphases include

(a) being physically active and engaging in activities that develop cardiovascular health, suppleness, muscular strength and endurance.

(b) an appreciation of how much partners contribute to learning.

Equipment needed

- 9 tennis balls
- stopwatch
- 3 hoops
- measuring tape
- 6 canes on 12 cones to form hurdles
- cones for circuit, throws

Warm-up activities

(1) Jogging is easy running with arms and heels low, usually with a regular 'one, two, three, four' rhythm.

(2) For the circuit speed practice, the arms and heels will come up higher from jogging style to running, with more forward incline of body, as you start to reach forward more with your strides.

Timed circuit

(1) Teacher guidance and coaching will have helped them to perform at appropriate bursts of 150-metre running speed in the warm-up. Wild, over-speedy sprinters will have been checked.

(2) An exact metre-wheel reading of distance when several metres wide of line will tell them how many extra metres this involves.

Class activity

(1) Landing after jumping on the hard playground must always be scaled down to 'short long' or 'low high' for safety, but the learning and understanding of the technique can still go ahead. Few strides are needed to reach 'half speed'.

(2) It helps to start run up with the eventual take-off foot.

(3) The 'mark' guide on the ground can be a line, mark, crack or light or dark patch.

Group activities

(1) We are (short) long jumping for style and controlled run-up, not length. The result will be about half of what they would do with a full run to a sand box landing area, but their understanding of the main features can still be gained.

(2) Partner marks and measures best of three throws – measuring where ball lands, not where it rolls. A jumping turn into the first of two, side-on steps, gives good forward transfer of weight into throw.

(3) Keeping a consistent approach to first hurdle at first line, every lesson, enables them to use a sprint start position of feet to bring them to clear first hurdle correctly every time. This also gives the momentum to do three strides between hurdles easily.

(4) Hoop throw is for accuracy as much as for distance. Release is with a straight arm in front of face at about 60 degrees. Aim to make it fly flat to land and settle, not roll away.

(5) Do one timed run only, and from a crouched spring start position, with no slowing down as they approach finish line – a common fault.

Partners, side lines touch relay

If second runner runs from a standing start in the first race and then a running start in the second and third races, the greatly improved times, being called out by the teacher, will show the class the importance of a running change-over in relays.

The teacher calls out the finishing positions of as many as possible.

Year 6 • May • Playground Lesson 3

LESSON PLAN • 30–50 MINUTES

WARM-UP ACTIVITIES   3–4 minutes

(1) Follow the leader with first leader showing partner three athletic skills you have enjoyed in our four-year programme, moving non-stop to warm up. He or she will be choosing from quick walking, jogging, running, long or high jumping, hurdling or triple jumping.
(2) New leader, can you join up these three athletic skills into a little sequence, maybe using jogging to link them together?

TIMED CIRCUIT OF 200 METRES   4–5 minutes

(1) Can you run on the spot to show me your idea of a sensible, 200-metre circuit speed that you think you can keep up all the way?
(2) As usual, we will go off in groups at 5 second intervals.

CLASS ACTIVITY; Relay baton take-over   5–8 minutes

(1) Baton in left hand, first runner. Run to pass it to partner who starts at first line, then runs to receive it near end of middle third area, offering inverted V of thumb and first finger. Go!
(2) Same order, offering to correct any over-early or late starts to 2's running. Are you using a check mark on the ground as a guide, running when your partner crosses it?
(3) (Change order. Practise twice. Race in each direction against other couples. Demonstration by good couples. Comments.)

GROUP ACTIVITIES; Five groups of six   15–28 minutes

(1) Relay practice, doing transfer within middle third of court. Both partners need to be aware of point at 10–12 metres where they plan take-over. Having practised, they race other couples.
(2) Scissors high jump over elastic 'bar' tied between high jump stands at 60 cm which is low enough to clear and land safely, but high enough to need correct technique. If 'bar' is hit, it does not matter because it does not impede.
(3) Large-ball throw with two hands starting above and behind head. 2-step approach to throwing line, accompanied by a strong backward bend of upper body, provides good forward weight transfer into throw. Partner marks and measures throw.
(4) Hop, step and jump after a short, 5 metre run to line. Aim to make all parts almost equal in length in a scaled-down triple jump. Even in this reduced practice we can learn the main features – consistent take-off from line; equal length hop, step and jump, spreading energy over whole event; landing from jump with both feet forward.
(5) Partner fun runs across width of court, to other side and back: (a) quick walking; (b) sprinting; (c) skipping; (d) three-legged race; (e) bowl a hoop; (f) any other good ideas.

TO END LINES AND BACK RELAY   3–5 minutes

Line 1 | X1 X2 X3 X4 X5 X6 | Line 2
In each of five teams, 1 runs to Line 1, turns and runs past own team on right-hand side to touch Line 2, turns and races back to give baton to 2 who has stepped out to right to receive baton in right hand. Race ends, after all have run, with 1 receiving baton from 6. Teacher calls out results.

The lesson's main emphases include

(a) Gaining consistency and skilful performance by thoughtful, planned practice.
(b) Encouraging pupils to be mindful of others; try hard to consolidate performances; recognise safety procedures for different activities.

Equipment needed

- 15 batons
- 6 hoops
- 6 skipping ropes
- 3 large balls
- measuring tape
- stopwatch for relays
- high jump stands and elastic 'bar'
- marker cones for throws and circuit

Warm-up activities

(1) The leader is 3 metres ahead to let follower see whole action including the approach. Following partner's take-off foot might be different in hurdles, jumps or triple jump.

(2) 'Little sequence' can be triangular – e.g. one side running, one side hurdling, one side hop, step and jump.

Timed circuit

(1) An easy, repeating jog/run, with relaxed hands, arms and legs reducing all tension, should be possible for the 200 metres by Year 6 pupils.

(2) They go off, after being told 'Remember start and finish times and keep near to the line of circuit. Group one, zero seconds, go! Group two, five seconds, go! Group three, ten seconds, go!' (etc.)

Class activities

(1) Incoming runner is responsible for the take-over, aiming baton at a steady, inverted V that does not move about. 'Running, running, reaching, taking' is their guide to timing.

(2) 'Mark on playground' is any line, crack, lump, or very dark or light mark, which is easy to see.
(3) 'Watch this demonstration and tell me the good points you noticed that we might learn from.'

Group activities

(1) When incoming runner passes check mark on ground, outgoing runner starts running so that baton will not stop moving. Both runners need to know that transfer is not expected or attempted before about 10 metres of running by outgoing receiver.
(2) Elastic 'bar' does not impede in any way or hurt shins. 'Bar' is kept low, 50–60 cm, to deter them from foolhardy, fast high jumping that is dangerous when landing on a playground surface. A 3- or at most 5-step approach run must be slow and carefully used.
(3) The long lever of straight arms, and body whipping backward and forward on a wide base with one foot forward, after the 2-steps approach, provides a powerful action. Aim throw high enough 'to let ball see its target at about 15–20 metres'.
(4) The usual fault is to do a very long hop, using all forward momentum, then a tiny step and a quick, short jump. If they practise saying 'Hop... and step...and jump.' with a three-equal-parts rhythm, a better, overall performance is achieved.
(5) Apart from the three-legged race where they work together, one partner races across court and back to touch partner who does the same.

To end lines and back relay

Runner with baton in left hand knows that receiving partner will be on the move. Both are expecting transfer of baton only when receiver has built up a good running speed, at about 10 metres. Teacher calls out results and times winner. Second race should be faster after the first practice.

LESSON PLAN • 30–50 MINUTES

WARM-UP ACTIVITIES   3–4 minutes

(1) Stand on one foot, lift and reach forward with other foot to 'paw' at the ground in front of you. Now, do the same again, but this time, lift your other knee and thigh higher before reaching out to paw at the ground; the second reach will be longer.
(2) Walk to first line. Jog to second. Run to third, emphasising a better knee and thigh lift than you normally use. Turn around and repeat back to start and I will look out for good running with a lively lift and reach in the forward leg to show you. (Demonstrations. Comments. Further practice to improve.)

TIMED CIRCUIT AND PART CIRCUIT OF 250 METRES   4–6 minutes

(1) This is our longest run in lessons and it needs to be planned sensibly. I want you to prove to yourselves how fit you are by completing the run, recovering quite quickly and feeling strong.
(2) For a change, group five will go off first. Zero seconds, go! Group four, five seconds, go!…

CLASS ACTIVITY; Bean bag put   5–8 minutes

(1) Partners stand 8–10 metres apart, one at a line. Stand side-on to each other, feet together, hand against neck as if you had the bean bag there. Elbow high to rear, weight over rear foot.
(2) Take a short step towards partner with nearer foot. Close other foot up to first foot, then take a long step to side with foot nearer partner, and go into your putting action, with arm moving straight forward into vigorous put.
(3) Try it, sharing one bean bag, having alternate puts. Step, close, step and put, using leg drive, body rotation, before arm push.

GROUP ACTIVITIES; Five groups of six   15–27 minutes

(1) Bean bag put with a chasse (step, close, step) into side-on position for the put forward from neck. Partner marks and measures best of three attempts.
(2) Standing high jump over low cane held loosely by partner. Jump can be from arm's length at front or side-on, close to cane. Partner can estimate vertical height jumped: 'about 60 cm'.
(3) 60-metre timed sprint, around a cone at 30 metres. They hope for improved times compared with April. One run only.
(4) Measured tennis ball throw with length of court the maximum, to contain the activity. Partner judges, marks and measures best of three throws. Starting back from line, they spring up and into a wide, side-on position with two strides for the throw with high bend of throwing arm over shoulder into stretch and throw.
(5) Hurdling over five sets of canes on pairs of cones, trying to keep up the 'over, 1, 2, 3, over' pattern of three steps running between hurdles. As they walk back to start, they can practise 'Hop…and step…and jump' to feel the equal parts.

ROUND THE CIRCUIT (ONE NETBALL COURT) RELAY   3–5 minutes

Three groups start at one court, two groups start at the other court, well spaced apart, standing inside line of court. 1s start race, just outside line, do a circuit and pass baton to next runner. All run once around court and race ends with 1 being given baton by last runner, 6.

The lesson's main emphases include

(a) Hoping that their recorded and obvious achievements and improvements will contribute to self-confidence.

(b) Practising to improve and refine performance, with increased control and accuracy.

Equipment needed

- 15 bean bags
- 3 tennis balls
- measuring tape
- 5 batons
- stopwatch
- high jump stands and elastic 'bar'
- marker cones for circuit and throws
- 6 canes and 12 cones for hurdles

Warm-up activities

(1) The increased forward reach of foot is quite marked when you lift knee and hip and feel yourself intentionally reaching forward each stride.

(2) If the same running rhythm is maintained and you add several centimetres to each stride, you must be running faster.

Timed circuit and part circuit

(1) A 250-metre run is a good test of endurance, fitness and ability to plan a longish run at a sensible speed that can be maintained.

(2) Remember to keep near the perimeter line to avoid adding extra metres to your run. Do not cut corners. Relax and do your best.

Class activity

(1) Without bean bag, they all practise the start position, side-on to line of put with wide stance. Forward arm is bent high as balance to body's backward lean.
(2) The 'step, close up, step', 'chasse' action aims to transfer the body weight forward to assist put.

(3) After chasse, they should feel rear leg drive, body rotation, arm thrusting forward from neck. Any movement back by putting hand is a throw and not allowed. Wrist snaps forward at end of put.

Group activities

(1) Practice is done slowly to feel the several parts, thinking about the technique. As they chasse forwards, they retain backward lean over rear leg; then rear leg drive, body turn, arm push.
(2) In standing high jump the emphasis is on a dynamic knees bend and stretch with feet together and a strong upward arm swing.
(3) In timed sprint, they are reminded of warm-up practice to encourage a good knee lift to increase stride length. Each runner is started, timed and told time, individually, by a team mate.
(4) Lots of practice is needed to co-ordinate the spring from left foot into a turn on to right foot, into a wide, side-on position with left foot well forward for tennis ball throw.
(5) Leading leg clears hurdle from front, going straight up, over and down into next stride. Other, trailing leg has to lift and bend to one side to take it over hurdle, before it pulls around and down.

Round the netball court relay

From marked team positions inside lines of court, each runner in turn steps forward, ensuring baton neither slows down nor stops.
Corners of circuit should be marked by cones to prevent tendency to cut corners. Well warmed up and practised, the team should do an even better time in the second race.

LESSON PLAN • 30–50 MINUTES

WARM-UP ACTIVITIES   3–4 minutes

(1) Walk briskly, side by side with a partner. When I call 'Go!' one of you show the other your running rhythm for the 300-metre run. After 15 seconds I will call out 'Walk!' When I call 'Go!' the second partner shows his or her 300-metre circuit speed.
(2) Freely, change between quick walking and short bursts of circuit speed running, trying to feel the right, sensible rhythm for you.

TIMED CIRCUIT AND PART CIRCUIT OF 300 METRES   4–6 minutes

(1) Keep relaxed in hands, arms and legs and feel a nice, easy rhythm as you run sensibly and test yourself and your fitness.
(2) I will call out '50 and 51 and 52', for example, where the 'and' means 0.5 seconds to give you a more accurate time.

CLASS ACTIVITY; Throwing tennis ball   5–8 minutes

(1) Partners, stand at opposite end lines of the netball courts. Show me a good jump into your side-on, 2-step throw. Spring and turn to side-on, throwing arm well back, then small cross-over step, then wide stride with other foot to throwing position. Arm starts well back, then bends to come over shoulder, stretching into throw, aiming at about 50 degrees.
(2) Throw for accuracy and medium distance, to no further than the opposite line. See if you can give your partner an easy catch.

GROUP ACTIVITIES; Five groups of six   15–27 minutes

(1) Tennis ball throw, judged, marked and measured by partner. Throw must not exceed length of court to contain the practice. Good examples of the jumping, turning, side-on action are shown.
(2) Team standing long jump with each in turn doing standing long jump from spot where previous jumper landed. Team distance is marked as challenge to other teams. Feet slightly apart, bend knees and swing arms behind. Drive forward with legs and swing arms forward. Bend knees to reach well forward. Next jumper stands in line with toes of previous jumper's landing place.
(3) Choice of 50- or 75-metre timed sprint. Timekeeper is always at same line. Runners start beside one of two cones, 25 metres apart for 2 x 25- or 3 x 25-metre run. Each takes turn as timekeeper.
(4) Scissors jump over elastic 'bar' tied between high jump stands at about 60 cm only. They use a low, springy, 3- or 5-step approach. Take-off is a rocking action along heel, ball and toes of jumping foot. Leading leg swings up and over bar strongly.
(5) Relay baton exchange with a partner, using middle third of court for transfer of baton. Both are planning to make exchange at 10–12 metres within third by which time both are running at speed. Baton passes form left hand to inverted V of receiver's reaching back, steady, right hand.

ROUND ONE NETBALL COURT RELAY   3–5 minutes

Teams are well spaced, using both courts, three at one, two at other with only one starting at each position. Because they are well spaced, there is no problem of some runners having to run wide and further. 'Take baton on the move in right hand. Relax and stride out well.' Results are called out by teacher who times both races as baton is passed back to first runner.

The lesson's main emphases include

(a) End of primary school reflection by teacher, thanking pupils for their consistently enthusiastic and wholehearted co-operation, and praising them for their improved results, increased fitness and skilfulness.

(b) Emphasising importance of fair play, honest competition and good sporting behaviour.

Equipment needed

- 15 tennis balls
- 5 batons
- stopwatch
- marker cones for relays and throws
- high jump stands and elastic 'bar'

Warm-up activities

(1) Partners should be able to advise, guide or restrain each other, aiming to feel the correct, sensible speed.

(2) The observing teacher suggests more or less speed as he or she watches them alternating their circuit running speed with quicker walking.

Timed circuit

(1) For this, their final timed circuit, the quicker runners can be bunched together to go off first on the clear 'track'.

(2) 'This is not a race against others. It is a time trial to let you check your sensible planning, stamina and powers of recovery.'

Class activity

(1) Learning the correct technique for transferring weight into a running throw will help their cricket and rounders fielding, both for distance and accuracy.

(2) Long throwing needs to be accurate, so the throw is limited to a court's length and must remain within a narrow sector to count.

Group activities

(1) Some Year 6 pupils will be able to throw enormous distances, but have to be limited during playground lessons. Cones at 5 metres apart help partner with distance or a tape can be used.

(2) On way back to team start line or a second effort, they can practise an easy hop, step and jump, trying to make them almost equal in length.

(3) They test themselves at a choice of distances, checking on one done often, or one done less frequently.

(4) Take off and landing on the playground means that a much scaled-down, safe and easy version must be insisted on to prevent any slipping back at take off or landing, or falling on a hand. Run up must be slow, bouncy, well-controlled, not fast nor out of control.

(5) Let them see how far they run while calling 'running, running, reaching, taking' before even offering to put right hand back to receive baton. It should be about 10 metres which is a good distance for getting into speed.

Round netball court relay

Planning, like performing and reflecting, are important elements within National Curriculum physical education, generally. Planning in athletic activities can be done within the relay baton exchange. Both runners plan to make baton exchange after at least 10 metres, by which time outgoing runner is moving at speed. Most primary pupils anxiously make the change over as soon as possible, often before second runner has even started to move. That team's baton is doing a stop-start journey with lots of interruptions to its forward progress.

LESSON PLAN • 30–50 MINUTES

WARM-UP ACTIVITIES   3–4 minutes

(1) In teams of six, walk at a good speed behind your leader. End person has to jog up to front to become new leader. When the new leader is in position, the next person jogs up to the front. Twice through, go!

(2) All change now to jogging behind the leader. End person now has to sprint to front to become next leader. Each end jogger must wait until new leader is in position. Twice through, go!

TIMED CIRCUIT OF 250 METRES   4–5 minutes

Plan to run or jog at a steady rhythm that you can keep up all the way. Do not sprint off fast at the start, leaving no energy for the finish, walking in and adding lots of seconds to your team score. Remember to subtract starting time from finishing time.

GROUP ACTIVITIES; Five groups of six   20–35 minutes

(1) Timed 75-metre sprint around cones at 25 metres apart. Each team member is timed individually by another team member who also starts the run. 'Set...go!' They try to finish fast, past line.

(2) Large-ball throw with each having best of three throws judged and measured by partner. Ball is held in both hands above and behind head. Two steps up to the line into the throw are permitted.

(3) Team standing long jump from a line. 1 jumps, lands and stands still so that 2 can line up toes with 1's as take-off place for team's second jump. Team result is marked for others to see and measured with the tape, parallel with jumpers.

(4) Hurdling over five hurdles (canes on pairs of cones) with three steps in between. Each has a 5 points start. If they clear first hurdle correctly, do the three rapid running strides in between, and do not knock any canes off cones, they keep all 5 points. Points are taken off for wrong take-off at first hurdle, for each wrong footwork in between hurdles and for any canes hit. Teacher advises on scoring.

(5) Bean bag put for partner to judge, mark and measure. Best put of four is measured. Putting partner may use the chasse (step to side, close feet, step to side) approach to side-on position from which to put from behind line. Hand stays against neck as rear leg drives forward, upper body rotates, and then hand and bean bag push forward into vigorous put. Hand with bean bag must not go backwards, away from neck – that is throwing and not allowed.

ROUND THE NETBALL COURT RELAY   3–6 minutes

Three teams stand ready inside lines of one court. Two teams are ready, equally well spaced inside the other court. 1 races around outside lines of own court and passes baton to 2 who has stepped outside the line, ready. Each team member races around the circuit and passes the baton to the next runner. The baton is received in the right hand, running to keep it travelling non-stop. The teacher calls out all finishing places and times.

Team Number _____

First place in activity gains five points for a team. Fifth place gains one point.

Event	Individual Results						Combined Result	Place 1st–5th	Points 5–1
	1	2	3	4	5	6			
250 m									
75 m									
Large ball throw									
Team long jump									
Hurdles									
Shuttle relay									
Total Points Position in Class									

LESSON PLAN • 30–50 MINUTES

WARM-UP ACTIVITIES   4–6 minutes

(1) Can you jog easily with small steps and feel a nice, steady rhythm? (Working on the straight.)
(2) Let your arms hang low. Heels do not touch the ground but they are also carried low. We want it all to feel relaxed.
(3) Can you now use the lines to show me little long and high jump actions as you check which foot you push off with, each time?

TIMED PART LAP OF 100 METRES   4–6 minutes

(1) Each group goes off at the time I call out which you must remember. Listen for and remember your finishing time.
(2) Number one group, zero seconds, go! Number two group, ten seconds, go! (After two groups have gone, incoming runners are given their times, then two more groups are sent off.)

CLASS ACTIVITIES   18–32 minutes

(a) Whole class tennis ball throw with a partner

(1) Stand, 3–4 metres apart, and throw underarm for an easy catch.
(2) Stand, one foot forward for good balance, and hold cupped hands forward as a target.
(3) Thrower, swing arm forward, back, then forward with a good aim.
(4) Move further apart, one step at a time, until you need to throw overarm. Stay in this position and do not move further apart.
(5) Stand, side-on to your partner, with throwing arm well back in a ready position. Bend and bring your arm high over your shoulder into your throw.

(b) Whole class relay race with a partner

(1) Stand side by side with your partner in centre of field. 1 races to touch inside lane of track, turns and races back to touch 2's hand. 2 races to touch opposite inside lane of track, then back to stand still, next to 1. Let's race. Number 1s, go! (Teacher calls results.)
(2) Well done. Let's have another race. You can speed it up by jumping into your touch and turn at the lines, and 2 can be crouched, ready to take off more quickly.
(3) For our last race, 2s will start. Remember your quick turns and crouching start. Go!

TEAM RELAYS   4–6 minutes

(1) For our shuttle relay, 1, 2 and 3 start at this line. 4, 5 and 6 start at this line.
(2) The baton is carried and received in the right hand. Don't move until you receive it. Each of you will run twice to bring you all back to your starting places. Go! (Teacher calls out finishing order and, ideally, the winning team's time.)
(3) Well done. One more race and see if we can beat the winner's time. Receivers, hold your hand still making a V between thumb and first finger for the passer to aim at. Go! (Well warmed-up, the winner's time is usually improved.)

The lesson's main emphases include

(a) Introducing the class to this new kind of lesson with its running, jumping, throwing, relays.
(b) Training the pupils to co-operate and respond readily to instructions to enable the lesson to flow with the minimum of 'dead spots' when no-one is moving.

Equipment needed

- 15 tennis balls
- 5 relay batons
- stopwatch

Warm-up activities

(1) The teacher explains the limits of the warm-up area. 'Stay on the track within these four marker ones.'
(2) The teacher can call out a suggested, slow, easy rhythm. 'Jog, two, three, four; easy, two, three, four; arms low, heels low.'
(3) Emphasise a 3-count run for the take-off in a scissors jump, at an angle to a line, and a 3- or 4-count run for a safe long jump.

Timed lap

(1) Class are told it will be 100 metres as they line up in their groups ready across the track. The teacher then goes to the finish line to start them with a shout, and to give them their finishing times.
(2) Because it is only a short run, only two starting times are possible because they will all be finished before 20 seconds. Therefore, other starts are needed for teams three to five. When finished, runners subtract finish times from start times to work out their exact times for recording back in class.

Class activities

Class Activities are easy to teach because all are being taught the same activity. Five different group activities, all at the same time, are more difficult to teach in a first lesson.

Within the throwing there will be opportunities for the whole class to 'Look at these two very good couples showing us their overarm throwing and catching. Watch them, then tell me what you think is very good in their performances'. Demonstrators and friendly, helpful comment makers are thanked by the teacher, then 'have another practice to see if you can use some of the good points seen and mentioned'.

In the whole class relay, they line up side by side, in the centre of the field, parallel to, and equidistant from the two straights of the track. The teacher (starter and judge) stands at one end of the line where he or she can see which couple finishes first.

Team shuttle relays

X5 X3 X1 | | X2 X4 X6

1 races to give baton to 2, and stay at the end of that line. 2 races to give baton to 3 and stays at end of 3's line. All run to the opposite side, then a second run takes them back to their own side to finish in their starting places. There should be time for two or three, timed and judged races with the teacher calling out the results. The baton is carried and received with the right hand.

Year 3 • April • Field Lesson 2

LESSON PLAN • 30–50 MINUTES

WARM-UP ACTIVITIES   3–4 minutes

(1) Follow your leader who will show you two or three lively, warm-up athletic actions (e.g. long and high jumps; hurdling; hop, step and jump).

(2) Can you join your athletic actions by jogging slowly and easily, mirroring each other?

TIMED PART LAP OF 100 METRES   3–5 minutes

Each group runs by itself, listening to its starting time, with groups one to three going off at five-second intervals, racing to the 100 metres mark where the teacher calls out the finishing times.

Groups four and five will be in a second race. Starting times are substracted from finish times to give race time.

CLASS ACTIVITY; Bean bag throw to partner   5–8 minutes

(1) Stand, 3–4 metres apart and throw underarm to your partner's outstretched cupped hands.
(2) Catching is as important as throwing. Watch it all the way into your hands, and let hands 'give' to stop it bouncing out.
(3) Well done. Now move back, one step at a time until you have to throw overarm, then don't move any further back.
(4) Your arm starts well back, then try to feel your back leg push, your body turn and, finally, the pull and throw as your arm bends and comes high over your shoulder. Leg; body; arm actions.

GROUP ACTIVITIES; Five groups of six   16–28 minutes

(1) Bean bag aiming at a hoop on the ground from 4–5 metres. Each partner has three bean bags and competes against his or her own partner.
(2) Timed 50-metre sprint, one runner at a time being timed. Each one takes turn at starting and timing, telling the runner their time before going to the start of race to await their turn; then running and being timed.
(3) Standing high jump over a low cane held by a kneeling partner. A 3-count run in at an angle to the cane starts with the foot that is also the take-off foot. Kneeling partner checks that leg nearer cane swings up and over cane.
(4) Rugby ball pass and follow across 3 metres.

     X5 X3 X1 | | X2 X4 X6

1 passes to 2 and runs to the end of the opposite line. 2 passes to 3 and runs to the end of opposite line, and so on until all are back in their own starting places.
(5) Race across 20 metres with each member of group taking a turn as starter. (a) quick walking; (b) sprinting; (c) skipping; (d) simple race created by the group.

SIDE-TO-SIDE RELAY RACES WITH A PARTNER   3–5 minutes

Same race as in the September lesson. Partners stand side by side in the middle of the field, mid-way between nearer lanes of both straights of track. On signal, 1 sprints to touch inside line of track on own side, then sprints back to touch 2 who sprints to touch own side line. Teacher calls out results as couples finish, and times winners. Race again with other partner starting and look for improved times.

LESSON NOTES • 3 LESSONS DEVELOPMENT

The lesson's main emphases include

(a) Re-introducing the class to the pattern of a busy athletic activities lesson, and the importance of immediate responses.

(b) Throwing for accuracy and working sensibly and safely, alone, in pairs and in groups.

Equipment needed

- 18 bean bags
- 6 skipping rops
- 3 hoops
- 3 canes
- 1 rugby ball
- stopwatch

Warm-up activities

(1) Groups are limited to designated, restricted area of the track and the field within it. No wandering off!

(2) Continuous jumping, bounding or hopping is far too difficult and needs to be broken up with the contrasting, easy jogging.

Timed part lap

If there is a straight 100 metres marked out, this speeds up the organisation. Pupils are in groups at one end line. The teacher, with a stopwatch, is at the other end line. Teacher calls out 'Twelve...and thirteen...and fourteen...and fif- teen' as they sprint past him or her. The 'and' represents 0.5 seconds for greater accuracy. If subtraction is a problem, start at no seconds and ten seconds for easier mathematics.

Class activity

Because catching is easier than with a ball, and because the bean bag does not bounce and run away, almost non-stop practising can be achieved. Emphasise a good angle of about 60 degrees in the overarm throw for distance and an easy catch, and encourage them to feel 'Leg push, upper body turn, arm bends high over, and throw!'

Group activities

An even number of six is recommended to allow for partner work.

(1) Bean bag aiming can be competitive between partners, best of three, or pairs, best of six. 'Throw it high enough to let it see the target.'

(2) Timed 50-metre sprint needs some class instruction on how to work the stopwatch; how to shout 'Set...go!' when starting the next runner; and when exactly to stop the watch and read it.

(3) Standing high jump over a low cane can be practised facing the cane at arms length from it, or standing beside it. A big arm swing above the head, then a knees bend to take arms behind, then a strong swing up and over with arms helping by swinging upwards.

(4) Rugby ball pass and follow is like a shuttle relay. Team can be challenged 'How many passes can you make in half a minute?' or team time can be taken for all to start and finish in same places.

(5) Short, fun races across 20 metres, only, have one of group taking a turn to say 'Set...go!'. One who is starter also tries to call out winners and runners-up names as they finish. This is one activity lending itself to the challenge 'Can your group invent a good fun, interesting, 20-metre race?'

Side to side relays with a partner

Times can be improved by speeding up the turn by jumping into it to be crouched, ready to sprint back to touch partner who should be in a crouched position ready to speed away. Times are checked and called out each time.

LESSON PLAN • 30–50 MINUTES

WARM-UP ACTIVITIES   3–4 minutes

(1) Group one leading, walk along a line on the track to first cone, thinking 'Straight' of your arms as they swing straight forward and backward , parallel with the line. Jog to second cone, feeling legs and arms moving straight ahead. Then run to pass third marker, feeling your shoulders, arms and legs moving straight ahead. (2) Same again back to the starting line, feeling that you are travelling down a narrow alley and having to keep straight to avoid bumping into the side walls. Walk; jog; run…go!

TIMED PART LAP OF 150 METRES   3–5 minutes

(1) I will shout to start you, group by group, from the finish where I will call out your finishing times which you must remember. Aim for a steady rhythm that you can maintain all the way. Group one, zero seconds, go! Group two, five seconds, go! (etc.)
(2) Sit down, relax and work out your time by subtracting the start time from the finish time. Tell me if you need help with the mathematics!

CLASS ACTIVITY; 3-steps scissors jump over low cane   5–8 minutes

(1) One partner will pick up a cane, carry it point down in front of them, find a space, kneel down and hold the cane at about 50 cm off the ground. (2) Jumper, come in at an angle to the bar with swinging leg nearer to the bar. Practise to see which is your jumping foot.
(3) Partner, help by checking that your partner is pushing with the foot further from the cane.
(4) Change over, now, please, to let the other partner work out his or her take-off foot.

GROUP ACTIVITIES; Five groups of six   16–28 minutes

(1) 3-steps scissors jump over low cane held by partner. Have four turns, then change over, checking each other's action.
(2) Partners relay on track. 1s race to pass baton to 2s at 20 metres. 2s race to the line at 40 metres, have a few seconds rest before racing in the opposite direction, back to the start.
(3) Bean bag put with a partner. Each has three puts with partner marking the best result with a cone. From a side-on position with the bean bag against neck, the action is a leg drive, then a body turn, then a push of the bag straight forward from the neck, high.
(4) 50-metre timed sprint on part of the track. Each takes a turn at starting and timing from the end of the run; telling the runner the time, then going to the start of run position and having own sprint timed.
(5) Partners, standing long jump. 1 does a standing long jump from the side of the track and stands still. 2 stands at the point where 1 landed and does the next jump across track. They continue alternating their standing long jumps to see how many are needed to take them to the other side-line. Repeat back.

SIX IN A LINE RELAY   3–5 minutes

    Line 1   X1 X2 X3 X4 X5 X6 | Line 2
1 races to touch Line 1, turns, races back to touch Line 2 and races back to give baton to 2 who repeats run. Relay ends with last runner, 6, giving the baton to 1.

LESSON NOTES • 3 LESSONS DEVELOPMENT

The lesson's main emphases include

(a) Appreciating how much help we receive from a partner in learning athletic skills and measuring performances.

(b) Practising to improve and refine techniques and performance in running and jumping.

Equipment needed

- 15 canes
- 9 bean bags
- 6 batons
- stopwatch
- marker cones for 50-metre sprint, bean bags throw and relays

Warm-up activities

(1) Groups line up across track, standing on a line which is a good visual guide for level of straightness.

(2) On the return run the teacher looks out for good examples with whom to demonstrate the meaning of 'straightness'.

Timed part lap

Teacher lines them up ready at the start, then hurries to the finish line, from which to shout 'Group one, no seconds, go!' and so on, and to call out finish times. Some will finish before 20 seconds, so last group go off as a second race.

Class activity

A demonstration straight away by the teacher, or soon after the start by a good pupil, is essential to show meaning of 'foot further from the cane jumps, and leg nearer cane swings up and over'.

After they jump and land, they can turn and come back on diagonal from opposite side, repeating the 3-step approach.

Group activities

With four groups of partner activities, it is important to have even numbers in groups, ideally of six.

(1) The class activity is one of the five groups to let pupils 'practise, improve and refine their performance' of the skill.

(2) In a group of six, three line up, holding the baton at the start. One of the group calls 'Set...go!' and they race to pass the baton to the stationary partners who race to the end line. They rest, then race back to pass baton to partners who race to start line.

(3) Much demonstrating is needed to show how the bean bag starts pressed against neck. A 'put' starts from the neck and travels forward. If bean bag travels back to behind the head, it is a throw.

(4) All except the timekeeper line up at the start of 50 metres. One at a time, they race to 50-metre line after timekeeper calls out 'Susan, set...go!' and Susan's time is taken as she passes the timekeeper. Susan is told her time and she stays to start and time the next runner.

(5) The width of the track is a good distance to check against, needing five or six good springs from a standing position. Each jumper performs from in line with the toes of the previous jumper's landing position. Toes slightly apart, high swing of arms, arms swing down and behind with a good knee bend, then the dynamic spring with arms swinging forward to help.

Six in a line relay

Baton is carried in left hand and runners run on right side of team line. Next runner steps to right side of team, holds right arm back with an inverted V between thumb and first finger. Baton is taken standing still, passed up into V by incoming runner.

Runner swaps baton from right hand to left for the change-over. Results and times should be called out for the two or three races for which time should be made.

LESSON PLAN • 30–50 MINUTES

WARM-UP ACTIVITIES
3–4 minutes

(1) Groups spread across track jog from first marker cone to second. Then they run with good lift of heels, knees, and arms to finish fast past the line of the third cone.

(2) Rest and recover for a few seconds, then back again, jogging and finishing fast. The good knee lift aims to give you a bigger stride to move you well forward with each step. Lift and reach.

TIMED PART LAP OF 150 METRES
3–5 minutes

(1) Each group will go off at 5 second intervals. Listen for your starting time and your finishing time. Run at your own sensible, comfortable, 'cruising speed' and ignore how others are running. Group one, no seconds, go! Group two, five seconds, go! (etc.)

(2) Sit down, recover, and subtract your starting time from your finishing time. Ask for help if you need it in subtracting.

(3) How do you feel? Do you know why you are hot and breathing deeply? Let's check times.

CLASS ACTIVITY; Relay baton exchange
5–8 minutes

(1) One partner holds baton in left hand, standing on this line. Other partner, stand in line with your partner on this next line, with your back towards them, holding right hand back, with an inverted V of thumb and first finger for your partner to aim at.

(2) 1, jog and hand baton to 2 who is standing still. 2, jog to my third line, stop and turn around for the next practice. Get ready, 2s with baton in left hand; 1s with right hand back, inverted V ready for the baton. Jogging, go!

(3) This time, when you take baton, be moving slowly forward to keep it just moving from start to finish. Start moving, receiver, when your partner passes a mark on the ground about 4 metres behind you.

GROUP ACTIVITIES; Five groups of six
16–28 minutes

(1) Relay baton exchange practice. 1s from first cone. 2s receive moving forward from second cone, jog to third cone, turn and rest for a few seconds. Final practices can be at speed, racing other couples to finish fast and first.

(2) Large-ball throw with a partner marking where it lands. Throw is from standing, with ball starting behind head.

(3) High jump over low elastic 'bar' tied between high jump stands. 3-step approach with same foot starting and taking off.

(4) 50-metre, timed sprint on straight of track. Each one has a turn at starting/timekeeping; telling runner the time; going to start of run position; sprinting to be timed.

(5) Throwing tennis ball for accuracy in threes. Hoop is held high by one and other two aim to throw the ball through it to each other for a catch. Rotate after six attempts and compete against another three for a 'best of 18 throws'. Throw 3 metres away from hoop.

RELAY RACE ROUND TRACK
3–5 minutes

Team members, numbered one to six, go to stand beside the marker cones which are numbered one to six, at equal distances round track. Baton is received, moving forward as practised in class activity. 6s, with baton at end, start next race.

LESSON NOTES • 3 LESSONS DEVELOPMENT

The lesson's main emphases include

(a) Demonstrating when asked; looking at demonstrations; making friendly, helpful comments about the work seen.

(b) Developing basic techniques in running and relays, and throwing for distance and accuracy.

Equipment needed

- 15 batons
- 9 large balls
- 3 tennis balls
- 3 hoops
- stopwatch
- marker cones
- high jump stands and elastic 'bar'

Warm-up activities

(1) Jog half way, then accelerate past end line marker. Lively, reaching leg action with dynamic arm swing.

(2) Low knees reduce stride length. Think 'knees lift' for speed.

Timed lap or part lap

(1) On some small fields, 200 metres will be a one-lap activity. On others, it will be a big part of the lap. We must avoid pupils distressing themselves by running too fast. We want an 'easy rhythm; easy rhythm; easy, 2, 3, 4; nice 'n easy'.
(2) Some in groups two and four, subtracting five and fifteen seconds from their finishing time, might need mathematical assistance.
(3) Big leg muscle action uses much energy, raising body temperature and increasing action of lungs to take in extra oxygen.

Class activity

(1) Teacher demonstrates the 'inverted V' of thumb and first finger of right hand, held still for easy baton exchange.
(2) A stationary change-over for first practices to let both feel the desired action – up into the V with receiver passive.
(3) The teacher can demonstrate the 'slowly moving forward' change-over with receiver passively a steady, inverted V target.

Group activities

Even number groups of six are the ideal.
(1) Further relay practice concentrates on 'Running, running, reaching, taking', starting to run as partner passes mark on ground – stone, weed, long piece of grass, crack, bare patch.
(2) Each has three throws, one foot in front of the other for good balance. Aim high enough for a good carry. Best throw is marked.
(3) Low elastic bar 'gives' and bounces back if you hit it, saving much time and preventing pained shins. Jumping foot is one further from bar, with nearer leg the one swinging up.
(4) The 50-metre sprint should be expertly carried out following its introduction and practice in September. Emphasise 'Finish fast', right past the timekeeper, as in our warm-up practices.
(5) Underarm aiming through vertical hoop, held high above head by third person, can be from any comfortable distance for throwing and catching.

Relay race round track

If groups of six are traditional in the school, it is a good idea to have six starting places clearly marked just inside the track. Runners are told to try to 'take the baton on the move in your right hand with its inverted V between thumb and first finger'.

Because the outside runners are on a wide arc, they run further than those on the inside. For the second race change the positions to let the outside teams run on the inside.

LESSON PLAN • 30–50 MINUTES

WARM-UP ACTIVITIES   3–4 minutes

(1) Jog, side by side, with a partner. One will set the rhythm for the pair, trying to show partner the steady rhythm used for one lap.
(2) (After 15 seconds) The other partner now sets the rhythm, trying to remember and show his or her, easy speed for the one lap.
(3) After a short rest, both have a last turn at setting the continuous, steady rhythm that they think is good for a one-lap run.

TIMED LAP OR PART LAP OF 200 METRES   4–5 minutes

(1) I want you all to improve, week by week, in your times for this, our longest run this year. So, take your time, and run at an easy speed that you can keep to. It is not a race; it is a time trial to see if you can spread your effort and keep going sensibly and happily for 200 metres.
(2) Groups of six, listen for your starting and finishing times. Group one, zero seconds, go! Group two, five seconds, go! (etc.)

CLASS ACTIVITY; Tennis ball throw   5–8 minutes

(1) Stand 4 metres apart and throw underarm for an easy catch.
(2) Catcher, hold both hands forward, cupped, and watch the ball all the way into your hands.
(3) Take one step back at a time until you need to start throwing overarm and higher. Then do not move any further back.
(4) Thrower, stand side-on to your partner, with your throwing arm well back. Throw by bending your arm to bring it over your shoulder before stretching into your throw and follow-through.

GROUP ACTIVITIES; Five groups of six   15–28 minutes

(1) Tennis-ball throw. Each partner has three throws. The other partner marks the best one with a cone. Target lines can be marked at 5-metre intervals as a help to the measuring partner.
(2) Relay change-over within a 20-metre, marked area. 1 runs to pass to 2 who uses take-over area to get into running strides before receiving baton. 2 sprints fast past the end line or cones. Both have a short rest, then repeat back to start line.
(3) Measured standing long jumps. Two-metre sticks parallel with the direction of jump are used to tell the jumper his or her result. Each jumps, is told the distance, watches the next jump and tells the result. On the way back to the next jump they can practise a hop, step and jump with equal parts.
(4) Gentle hoop throw for direction to a partner. Partners stand 15 metres apart, side-on when throwing. Use long discus action, to land it just in front of partner, feeling the back leg push, then the shoulder turn, then the throw with straight arm at about shoulder height.
(5) Fun races over 20 metres: (a) quick walking; (b) sprinting; (c) skipping; (d) bowling a hoop; (e) invent a simple good fun race.

RELAY RACE AROUND TRACK   3–5 minutes

Team members are numbered 1 to 6, with 1 starting the race and 6 finishing it. Within the lesson's two races, and week by week, the inside-of-track position with the shortest run is rotated for fairness.

Six start positions should be marked by cones.

LESSON NOTES • 3 LESSONS DEVELOPMENT

The lesson's main emphases include

(a) Enjoying a varied, interesting and challenging lesson, particularly now when it is running smoothly, almost non-stop.

(b) Measuring, comparing and improving own performances.

Equipment needed

- 15 tennis balls
- 5 batons
- 3 hoops
- 2 metre sticks
- stopwatch
- cones to mark throws and relay starts

Warm-up activities

(1) They have to imagine that they are doing a one-lap run, and plan what is an appropriate speed that they can manage all the way round.

(2) The hoped-for outcome of both trying to set a rhythm is a speed that is sensible and not the usual, too fast at the start.

Timed lap or part lap

(1) Emphasise that a steady, easy, repeating rhythm run is what is wanted – not a dash away at the start and a tired, walking finish.

(2) If any express great problems with their subtraction, they can go off at the start 'First group zero seconds, go!'.

Class activity

(4) The standing tennis ball throw should be done to the teacher's command – balls will fly all over the place if it is not controlled. '1s, ready, lean back and throw! 2s, collect the ball and stand on your line, ready. 2s, let arm bend high over your shoulder. Ready…throw!

Group activities

(1) As always, the class activity is included among the five groups for more practice to enable them to improve their performance, and to have a best distance measured.

(2) The incoming runner carries the baton in the left hand at speed. The receiving partner looks for partner crossing a suitable check mark on the ground at 4–5 metres behind him or her, then starts running. Right arm is back and steady with inverted V of thumb and first finger waiting for baton. Pairs can race pairs both ways, after a short rest.

(3) A distance of 2 metres, marked by 2-metre sticks, beside the jumping area, will be enough to serve all levels of jumping from a standing start with feet slightly apart.

(4) Thrower stands side-on to partner, with hoop held in straight arm out to rear. A long-arm, slinging, discus-like action brings hoop, around arm at shoulder height, to a point straight ahead where it is released at about 45 degrees.

(5) An efficient starter/judge can shout out names in the order they pass the finish line from which he or she starts and judges. Starter calls out 'Set…go!' and they must be still on 'Set'.

Relay races around track

Each stays at the mark at which they made the baton exchange, one position on in the race. The second race will have 6s starting because they have the batons from the first race. Each team's time can be called out by the teacher to give all the pleasure of an improved time.

LESSON PLAN • 30–50 MINUTES

WARM-UP ACTIVITIES   3–4 minutes

(1) Jog easily, keeping within these four cones on the track. Let arms and legs be completely relaxed with no stiffness.
(2) Move a little faster now, running tall with a good uplift of heels, knees, arms and head.
(3) If I call 'One!' find one line to stand on, balanced. If I call 'Two!' be still with feet wide and standing on two lanes. Let's see who is first... One! (Teacher names winners)
(4) Off you go, running again and listening... Two! (Repeat)

TIMED PART LAP OF 150 METRES   4–5 minutes

To assist subtraction of starting time from finishing time, two teams at a time, only, go off at zero seconds and ten seconds, necessitating three runs – groups one and two; three and four; and five by itself. Everyone's time will be noted for the competition.

GROUP ACTIVITIES   20–35 minutes

(1) Timed 50-metre sprint. Teams will shout encouragement to one another to inspire a best-ever time for the team score.
(2) Team standing long jump. From a start line to be used by all groups, the leader does a standing long jump, then stands still. Second jumper stands in line with leader's toes, does his or her jump and stands still to let third jumper see where to start from. The distance reached by the last jumper in the team is marked clearly or can be measured by the teacher.
(3) Bean bag aiming into a hoop in threes. Each member of the three (half of team) has three bean bags and aims to land them inside the hoop from a marked line at about 5 metres. The better of the two half-team scores is recorded.
(4) Non-scoring practice at high jump stands with elastic 'bar' at a low, safe height all can clear. 3-count run in to do scissors jump with foot further from bar, and to swing up with foot nearer the bar.
(5) Tennis ball throw with partner marking and measuring the best of four attempts from a standing position. Partner marks where the ball lands, not where it rolls to. Teacher will decide how to measure.

TEAM SHUTTLE RELAYS; 30 metres   3–6 minutes

            X5 X3 X1 | | X2 X4 X6
1 races to hand baton to 2. 1 stays at back of 2's line while 2 races to hand baton to 3 and stays at back of line. Two runs each brings baton back to 1 from 5 to end race. Baton is carried and received in right hand. Teacher calls out results, first to fifth, and times the winning team.

Team Number _____

First place in activity gains five points for a team. Fifth place gains one point.

Event	Individual Results 1	2	3	4	5	6	Combined Result	Place 1st–5th	Points 5–1
150 m									
50 m									
Standing long jump									
Bean bag aim									
Tennis ball throw									
Shuttle relay									
								Total Points Position in Class	

LESSON PLAN • 30–50 MINUTES

WARM-UP ACTIVITIES · 3–4 minutes

(1) Jog 10 metres to the first marker cone. Run to the next 10-metre marker, noting which foot strikes the line. Then run at a brisk speed to the third marker, counting number of strikes for the starting foot to reach the line. Jog on to the last marker.
(2) When you go back this time, can you lift your knees to give you a longer stride and see if you can run the middle part with fewer strides. Jog; run and count; jog; off you go!

TIMED PART LAP OF 150 METRES · 4–5 minutes

(1) Travel at something between the jog and the brisk run you have just practised. I want you to feel not too worn-out by your run.
(2) Groups go off at 5 second intervals. Please note your starting time, and remember it and your finishing time which I will call out. Group one, zero seconds, go! Group two, five seconds, go! (etc.)

CLASS ACTIVITY; Throwing a large ball · 5–8 minutes

(1) Partners stand, 3–4 metres apart for an easy, two-handed throw for accuracy. The chest pass with hands at sides of ball, thumbs back, fingers spread, is snapped at partner's outstretched hands. They can try the two-handed pass that starts with the ball just above one shoulder.
(2) Now move back to a distance from which you can throw the ball further with straight arms above and behind the head. It must be a con-trolled, accurate throw for your partner to catch.

GROUP ACTIVITIES; Five groups of six · 15–28 minutes

(1) Large-ball, 3–4 metres throw for accuracy, bouncing ball with chest or shoulder throw into hoop for partner to catch. Then 8–10 metres apart for a longer, overhead throw and catch.
(2) Standing high jump over a low cane held by partner. Jumper can stand facing cane at arms length, or start side-on to cane. A good knee bend with swing back of arms is followed by a strong drive from legs and upward swing of arms.
(3) 50-metre sprint times will be interesting to compare with their Year 3 times. Each pupil takes turn at starting/timing one runner; then going to start a run; then taking turn at the run.
(4) Relay baton change-over, on the move, with-in a marked 20-metre area. The three pairs can compete against one another with one of the group calling out 'Set…go!' After running one way, they rest for a few seconds, then change over duties racing the other way. Encourage call-ing 'Running, running, reaching, taking' for take-over that keeps the baton moving.
(5) Partner fun runs across 20 metres. One races to 20-metre line, turns, races back to touch partner who does the same. (a) quick walks; (b) sprinting; (c) skipping; (d) invent a simple fun run.

SHUTTLE RELAYS; 30 metres apart · 3–5 minutes

        X5 X3 X1   X2 X4 X6
1 runs to pass baton to 2 and stays at back of 2's line. 2 races to pass it to 3 and stays at back of line. All run and stay, there and back, finishing in own starting positions. Carry and receive with right hand. Receiver must stand still until baton is received.

LESSON NOTES • 3 LESSONS DEVELOPMENT

The lesson's main emphases include

(a) Responding readily to instructions; being physically active; and being mindful of others.

(b) Refining basic techniques in running and relays, and throwing for distance and accuracy.

Equipment needed

- 15 large balls
- 5 batons
- 3 canes
- stopwatch
- marker cones for warm-ups, fun runs and relays

Warm-up activities

(1) We want them to appreciate how a better knee and thigh lift contributes to greater stride length.

(2) Several extra centimetres on each stride take you nearer the finish than the old, shorter strides did, and they speed you up.

Timed part lap

(1) Year 3 experience and practice should be paying off now in better striding speeds over these part lap distances. No-one should be dashing off at speed and finishing, walking and weary, as in their earlier, inexperienced efforts.

(2) Check that they can manage the subtraction of starting time from finishing time. Mathematic problem cases can go off at 'zero seconds' which makes their finishing time their part-lap time.

Class activity

(1) In the chest pass the hands are up and the elbows are down, with arms bent at the start.
(2) The whole of the upper body should feel that it is coming into this longer throw. The feet are well split, one forward, one back.

Group activities

(1) The class activity, as always, is included among the group activities to enable them to practise it for increasing control and accuracy.
(2) Partner holds cane at a safe but challenging height for the jumper. It will be held loosely in case partner hits it.
(3) Class will need a reminder of the correct way to start the race with a 'Set...go!' when the runner is ready and steady, and how to operate and read the stopwatch.
(4) Receiving partner crouches with back towards incoming partner, right arm back with inverted V of thumb and first finger ready to receive baton from partner carrying it in right hand. When 1 passes an appropriate mark on the ground at about 4 metres behind 2, 2 starts to run to receive the baton on the move.
(5) 'There and back, partner fun runs' are short and each couple takes a turn at starting the races fairly. Rules must be clear. 'In quick walking, there is always one foot touching the ground. Skip with your rope all the way. No walking, trailing rope and not skipping.' Invented races must be safe and simple.

Shuttle relays

'Look and see where you are at the start of the race. After your run to the opposite end, and your run back to the starting end, all will finish back in own starting position. Leader will hold baton above head as a finishing signal.'

They carry and receive baton in the right hand, showing the inverted V to the incoming runner who wants the hand to be a still target, not one that is moving about, pursuing the baton.

LESSON PLAN • 30–50 MINUTES

WARM-UP ACTIVITIES   3–4 minutes

(1) Follow your leader who will show you a mixture of running; hurdling and long jumping across lines on the track; scissors jumping at an angle to the lines.

(2) Keep practising, but remember your take-off foot in hurdling, long and high jumping might be different to your partner's.

TIMED PART LAP OF 150 METRES   4–5 minutes

(1) Seven months on from September's lesson with its timed 150 metres, there should now be an improvement in the times recorded. Seven months of the gymnastic activities, games and dance, to which all pupils are now entitled, should also have made a big contribution to their all-round fitness.

(2) Listen for your starting and finish times so that you can work out today's part-lap, 150 metres run. Group one, zero seconds, go! Group two, five seconds, go! (etc.)

CLASS ACTIVITY; Hurdling over canes on ground   5–8 minutes

Three sets of canes are placed on each lane on the ground, about 4 metres apart, starting at 10 metres from the start of the straight where groups line up behind one another.
(1) Run to your first cane and hurdle over it. Then continue on to the next two and hurdle over them. See which is the foot you like to lead with. Stay at the other end for your return run.
(2) This time, run and hurdle, trying to lead with the same foot each time by thinking 'Over, 1, 2, 3, over, 1, 2, 3'.

I have tried to help by putting the canes quite near each other.

GROUP ACTIVITIES; Five groups of six   15–28 minutes

(1) Hurdling, using two lanes, over three canes on low cones. All try to establish which is the take-off foot, using three steps in between to make it work smoothly.
(2) High jumping over elastic 'bar' set at low height for all to practise a 3-count run-up, starting run up and jump, using same foot. 'Left, right, left and jump, or right, left, right and jump.'
(3) Tennis ball throw with a partner. Each thrower can have three turns and partner marks the best of three, marking where the ball landed, not where it rolled. Throwing area should have a throwing line and lines at 5 metres apart as a quick guide.
(4) Three in a team relay for two teams. 1 runs to pass baton to 2 at 20 metres. 2 runs on to pass baton to 3 at 40 metres. 3 runs on to touch line at 60 metres, turns and runs back to 2, still at 40 metres mark. 2 runs back to pass to 1 at 20 metres mark. 1 runs to finish race at start line.
(5) Bean bag put with a partner marking best of three puts.

TEAMS OF THREE, THERE-AND-BACK RELAY   3–5 minutes

Each group of six has an 'A' and a 'B' team of three runners. Because there are ten teams, the race will be across the field, track straight to far side, track straight, and back again. 1 passes to 2 who passes to 3 who runs to end line, turns and runs to pass back to 2 who runs to pass to 1 who races to finish at start line and the timekeeping, judging teacher.

LESSON NOTES • 3 LESSONS DEVELOPMENT

The lesson's main emphases include

(a) Working wholeheartedly at activities that develop cardiovascular health, strength and endurance.

(b) Practising hard to perform with greater control and consistency.

Equipment needed

- 18 canes
- 12 cones
- 9 bean bags
- 6 batons
- 9 tennis balls
- high jump stands and elastic 'bar'

Warm-up activities

(1) The easy steady-rhythm running is the main content to be interspersed with hurdling over a line, long jumping from a line, and easy, three-step scissors jumps approaching a line at an angle of 45 degrees.

(2) After this practice, they can be asked 'Show me the foot that leads your hurdling. Lift the foot that leads your long jump. Lift the foot that swings up first in your high jump'.

Timed part lap

(1) Before they start, emphasise that tension, even in the way they hold their hands while running, can spread to arms and shoulders, neck and chest. Let them practise standing, swinging arms forward and back, loosely. Then let them feel the difference when their hands, then arms, then shoulders and neck become tight.

(2) Relax arms and upper body. Feel that you are running at an easy, steady speed that you can keep up. Remember to subtract start time from finish time.

Class activity

(1) Three canes are laid down on the ground in each of the six lanes, and each group in turn practises running over the canes to check which is their take-off foot that goes up and over and down straight on to the track again.

(2) Explain 'To let you lead with the same leg each time, you need to feel – leading leg over, then stride, stride, stride, then leading leg over again. Over, 1, 2, 3, over, 1, 2, 3, over'.

Group activities

(1) The class activity hurdling continues, developed by raising height of canes on low cones, for realism. Good performances can be demonstrated before they rotate to next place.

(2) By now, they should know whether they are right or left foot jumpers and practise from an angle of 45 degrees with jumping foot further from 'bar'.

(3) Throwing for distance and accuracy with partner collecting the three balls and judging the best one by referring to distance guides, lines, markers or tape.

(4) Because distance covered is small, ask them to take baton standing still in inverted V made by thumb and first finger.

(5) Putting, not throwing. Bean bag starts against neck and only moves forward into straight arm push. Any backward movement by hand becomes a throw which is not allowed.

There-and-back relay

Teacher stands at the start and finish line to call out winners and runners-up, and to time winners. Transfer of baton is helped if receiver is passive, holding hand back, steady, to give incoming runner a still target. There should be time for three, timed races.

LESSON PLAN • 30–50 MINUTES

WARM-UP ACTIVITIES   3–4 minutes

(1) Walk to first marker; jog to second marker; run at three-quarter speed to third marker, emphasising 'Straight ahead running'. Let feet, arms, shoulders and head keep on a straight-ahead path.
(2) Turn around and repeat back to start line. You can run on one of the lines to help you and me check on your straightness.

TIMED LAP OR PART LAP OF 200 METRES   3–5 minutes

(1) Because this month's distance is further than last month's, let your steady, repeating rhythm be a little slower for this first try. Feel relaxed, particularly in your hands and arms and, of course, keep as near to the inside line as possible.
(2) Please remember your start and finish times so that you learn your lap time to record in class later. Group one, zero seconds, go! Group two, five seconds, go! (etc.)

CLASS ACTIVITY; Relay baton exchange   5–8 minutes

(1) Let's practise across the field, from track straight to track straight. 1, hold baton in left hand. 2, half way across the space, show me your right arm extended well back showing an obvious, inverted V between thumb and first finger.
(2) Receive baton on the move, moving off when partner crosses a mark on the grass, 4–5 metres behind you. Ready? Go!

GROUP ACTIVITIES; Five groups of six   16–28 minutes

(1) Relay, running change-over practice transfers to the track and a 20-metre, marked, take-over area. Three pairs can race each other on the 40-metre run, with 10 metres before and after the take-over.
(2) Bean bag throw for distance and accuracy. Partners throw to each other's hoop target, at a distance of 15–20 metres. This is a standing, side-on, overarm throw.
(3) 50-metre timed sprint should produce some pleasing improvements compared with the previous September.
(4) High jumping over realistic 'bar' between high jump stands. A bouncy, 3-count run-up is looked for, followed by a high swing up of the leading leg which is one nearer the 'bar'.
(5) Throwing a hoop to a partner for accuracy and medium distance, about 20 metres apart. The discus style throw is from a side-on starting position with hoop held well back with straight arm. Hoop is pulled around at shoulder height and ahead of thrower.

SIX IN A LINE RELAY   3–5 minutes

Line 1 | X1 X2 X3 X4 X5 X6 | Line 2
Team lines up behind 1. 1 races to touch Line 1, turns and races to touch Line 2, turns and runs to give baton to 2 who repeats it all. Race ends when 6 passes baton back to number 1. Baton is received in right hand on right side of team lines. Teacher at front of line calls out results and times the two or three races.

LESSON NOTES • 3 LESSONS DEVELOPMENT

The lesson's main emphases include

(a) Enjoying the variety within these summer-term lessons in the fresh air with their running, jumping, throwing and relays.

(b) Throwing for accuracy and distance, and improving technique in running and jumping.

Equipment needed

- 6 batons
- 9 bean bags
- 6 hoops

- high jump stands and elastic 'bar'
- marker cones for warm-ups and relays

Warm-up activities

(1) The distance can be 10–15 metres for each of the walk, jog and runs. They will go there and back three or four times.

(2) There can be a demonstration of good straight ahead action, seen by teacher from front view as they come towards him or her.

Timed lap or part lap

(1) 200 metres is no marathon, but running it too quickly can leave a youngster distressed for the rest of the lesson.

(2) They should be encouraged to run as near to the inside of the track as possible. A wider arc extends the run beyond 200 metres.

Class activity

(1) Half, with baton in left hand, line up on the inside line of the track. Receiving partner stands, half way across centre area of track, with back towards partner, right arm back.

(2) Ask second runner to look for a mark on the grass behind them at about 4–5 metres. When incoming partner crosses that mark they move off to practise taking the baton on the move. Receiver is asked to reflect on whether they went off too early or late for a good take-over.

(3) Other partner starts practice back to original start line. Two races against all other couples can now be run.

Group activities

(1) Baton receivers should say to themselves 'Running, running, reaching, taking' to delay the take-over for about 10 metres of running.

(2) Each alternates throwing/aiming three bean bags with receiving/collecting. 'Aim high enough to let bean bag see the target.'

(3) Remind them of how to start, stop and read the stopwatch, and how to start the one runner. 'Set…go!'

(4) Run up is slow and bouncy, rather than fast. Last stride is a rock up from heel, ball and toes of foot further from bar.

(5) The hoop turn and throw starts with a drive from rear leg; then a turn of upper body and shoulders, pulling the hoop with a long arm action at about shoulder height; then the final slinging action as whole body finishes, facing the front and the target.

Six in a line relay

Teams line up, well separated with leader holding baton in left hand. Lines 1 and 2 are 20–25 metres apart, so each runner does a 40–50-metre run. Receiver takes the baton on the move, aiming to keep it moving from start to finish. While running the baton is transferred to the left hand. Teacher calls out order of finish and times the winning team for each of the two or three races.

LESSON PLAN • 30–50 MINUTES

WARM-UP ACTIVITIES   3–4 minutes

(1) Jog at a nice easy rhythm, side by side with partner. 'Feel' your rhythm, moving in unison. When you turn, the inside runner takes shorter strides, almost on the spot on a sharp turn.
(2) Now, can you jog, one behind the other with the front person trying to remember and repeat the jogging rhythm already done? When I call 'Change!' the following partner has to accelerate for a few strides to become the new leader, jogging again.

LAP OR PART LAP OF 200 METRES   4–5 minutes

(1) On most primary school fields, this will be a whole lap or a part lap to run well within oneself.
(2) Keep near the left side of the track so that you are not running further than necessary. It is important to know your time after this run. Listen carefully for your start time which you subtract from your finish time.

CLASS ACTIVITY; Throwing tennis ball   5–8 minutes

(1) Stand 4–5 metres apart for underarm throwing and catching.
(2) Catcher, hold both hands forward to give your partner a target to aim at. Let arms give and hands close around the ball for a secure catch.
(3) Move further apart until you need to start throwing overarm from a more side-on position.
(4) Let your arm bend to come high over your shoulder, then stretch into your throw and long follow-through aim.

GROUP ACTIVITIES; Five groups of six   15–28 minutes

(1) Partners, tennis-ball throw in marked throwing area. Each has three throws and partner marks the best.
(2) Partners, standing long jump. One starts with toes touching first line of track, does a standing long jump and stands still so the partner can jump from that landing place. They jump from standing start, alternately, to count number of leaps required to take them to the far side line of the track. They repeat and try to improve back to start, comparing own result with other couples.
(3) Hurdling down two lanes, each of which has three hurdles (canes on cones), checking take-off foot, then trying to lead with it over each hurdle. Pairs can race, side by side, to a line.
(4) Throwing a large ball across a 10-metre space, to clear heads and hands of another pair in the space. Pairs alternate throwing to each other with a turn in the middle. Use a two-handed, straight-arm throw from above and behind the head for the distance and the height needed to clear the reaching hands in the space.
(5) How far can you run in 5 seconds? One partner is challenged to tell marking partner where to stand on track as estimate of 5 seconds running distance. One of the marking partners calls 'Set…go!' and all the runners sprint off. On fifth second timekeeper shouts 'Now!' and the runners stop to see exactly how far they went. Change over places.

ROUND THE TRACK RELAYS   3–5 minutes

Ideally, the six starting positions are clearly, permanently marked, because all groups of six runners will use them often in these lessons. 1s start race and 6s are the last runners. 6s, still with batons, start the second race.

LESSON NOTES • 3 LESSONS DEVELOPMENT

The lesson's main emphases include

(a) Enjoying an interesting, almost non-stop lesson, and being praised for good quality listening and responding that permits this continuous action to take place.

(b) Responding enthusiastically to a variety of challenges.

Equipment needed

- 15 tennis balls
- 12 cones
- 6 canes
- 5 batons
- 2 large balls
- stopwatch

Warm-up activities

(1) The extent of the 'field classroom' will be explained. This area will contain the class, possibly on half of the track straight, in order to encourage much direction changing and turning.

(2) The accelerating partner leans into the more rapid striding to become leader, then returns to the normal jogging rhythm.

Timed lap or lap and part lap

(1) The well-practised, medium-speed jogging rhythm is a good guide to the speed to be tried over distance.

(2) They will not appreciate that the inside lane of the track is the 200-metre part, unless told. Outer lanes on an extended arc lengthen the distance.

Class activity

(3) The overarm throwing will start at about 15 metres, where they should all stay, so that the throwing will be reasonably controlled and straight. We are practising the side-on skill, not seeing how far we can all throw.

(4) A demonstration of a throw that starts well back, then bends to come high over the shoulder, is more helpful than long explanations. Watch! Try!

Group activities

(1) As in every lesson, the class activity, just practised, is included among the group activities. They now try out their skill in throwing for distance and having it measured – roughly, 'Between third and fourth cones', or to the nearest metre if a tape has been placed beside area.

(2) Stand with feet apart, toes slightly turned in. Bend knees and swing arms behind you. Drive forward with strong leg push and big arm swing. Body stretches out fully, then knees bend strongly to bring feet as far forward as possible for the landing.

(3) Leading leg goes straight up and over the hurdle and straight down on other side. Trailing leg lifts and bends up and out sideways, then pulls around and down to land in front of leading foot.

(4) The teacher adjusts the gap between throwers to let them throw up and over the opposition successfully.

(5) Their estimates of distance they can cover in 5 seconds will be inaccurate and over-optimistic and far less than the 40-plus metres they estimated.

Around the track relay

Because the inside runners are running a shorter distance than those running wider on the outside of the track, the starting positions for the second race should be reversed. Teams four and five will be on the inside and teams one and two will run on the outside. Three can stay in the middle.

LESSON PLAN • 30–50 MINUTES

WARM-UP ACTIVITIES   3–4 minutes

(1) Partners, side by side, practise quick walking with quick, bent-arm action, always ensuring that one foot is on the ground.
(2) Partners stand, side by side, down middle of field area within the track. Each does quick walk to touch nearer inside line of track, turns and walks back to finish beside partner. After the practice, there are several competitive quick-walk races against all other couples with teacher calling out the results.

TIMED LAP OR PART LAP OF 250 METRES   4–5 minutes

(1) Run; jog; or run and jog, keeping well to the left of the track to keep the distance as short as possible. Start at a sensible speed, well within yourself. It is not a race.
(2) To make the subtraction of starting time from finishing time easy, we will all go off at 10 second intervals. Group one, zero seconds, go! Group two, ten seconds, go! (etc.)

CLASS ACTIVITY; Scissors jump over low cane   5–8 minutes

(1) Partner with cane, find a good space, kneel down with one knee and one foot on the ground holding cane at height of higher knee.
(2) Jumper, take a 3-count run in and jump from foot further from cane. Leg nearer cane swings up into jump. After landing, stay on that side, turn around and repeat the whole movement.
(3) Partner, holding cane, watch your partner's action, and check it. After six jumps, change places.

GROUP ACTIVITIES; Five groups of six   15–28 minutes

(1) Scissors jump over elastic 'bar' tied to high jump stands. Take a 3-step run-in, starting run and pushing off into jump with same foot.
(2) 50-metre timed sprint, emphasising 'Good, straight action; good knees lift for stride length; and finish fast, running past timekeeper'.
(3) Putting a bean bag. Partner puts from outside line of track and has three attempts. Partner marks best of three with a dome cone. Bean bag must stay in contact with neck, and only go forward into put. If hand goes back, it is a throw and not allowed.
(4) Relay take-over practice within marked, 20 metres area. Pairs can race in one direction, rest, then race back to starting line. The baton change-over, into running receiver's right hand, should take place between 10 and 12 metres in take-over area.
(5) Partner, there and back, fun runs over 20 metres. Each pair can take a turn at being starter and judge in: (a) quick walking; (b) sprinting; (c) bowling a hoop; (d) skipping; (e) an invented fun run.

AROUND THE TRACK RELAYS   3–5 minutes

Let's have group five starting on the inside for the first race. Then teams four, three, two, and one will be on the outside. 1s, carry baton in left hand. All receive in right hand, on the move, then transfer baton to left hand for the run and hand-over. To receive, show incoming runner a good, inverted V between thumb and first finger and hold the right arm well back and still. Get set...go!

LESSON NOTES • 3 LESSONS DEVELOPMENT

The lesson's main emphases include

(a) Strong partner and group 'togetherness' and contribution to improved skilfulness and enjoyment of the lesson.

(b) Good sporting behaviour as individuals and team members, observing the conventions of fair play and honest competition.

Equipment needed

- 15 canes
- 9 bean bags
- 5 batons
- stopwatch
- cones for marking putting, fun runs and relays

Warm-up activities

(1) Body is upright with little forward lean in the quick walking. Bent arms move quickly to balance the quick little walking steps. There must be one foot on the ground at all times, or it becomes running.

(2) Explain race clearly. 'Walk to nearer straight of track; touch it with one foot; turn and walk back to partner. Set…go!'. Calling out results is important.

Timed lap or lap and part lap

(1) On most fields, 250 metres will be more than one lap. They will probably start at beginning of straight, do a circuit and finish at end of straight – not too worn out, we hope, because they have been sensible and spread their effort evenly over the whole run.

(2) The whole point of the run is to test oneself, find out one's time, and improve on it. Therefore, they must be clear about times.

Class activity

(1) A cane held loosely and low will not lead to accidents. A cane held high, leading to foolhardy, very high jumps from grass on to grass, will lead to bad slips and falls.

(2) The line, diagonally through the cane, is the approach line on both sides of the cane for the 3-strides jumper.

(3) Partner becomes the teacher, checking that the jumper is approaching the cane from an 45-degree angle; pushing with remote foot and swinging up leg nearer bar.

Group activities

(1) The same 3-stride approach is practised over the more realistic setting of stands and high jump 'bar'. Good examples of a slow, bouncy approach with a high, leading leg swing after a rock up on to heel ball and toes of jumping foot, should be demonstrated.

(2) Comparison with September's time will be interesting, and, it is hoped, encouraging, and a clear proof of improved cardiovascular health, fitness and strength.

(3) Lines of track, usually 1 metre across, give a quick guide to distance gained. A demonstration of the correct, non-throwing action is essential.

(4) Receiver should say 'running, running, reaching, taking' as guide to covering about 10 metres before offering right hand to receive baton. Incoming runner should understand this plan.

(5) These short, good fun competitions can be expanded by asking 'Can you plan any other simple fun races for others to share?'

Around the track relays

Group starting positions on the track are reversed in fairness to group five who usually start and run on the outside, longer arc of the track. Any team, badly beaten in the first race, can be on the inside for the second race.

LESSON PLAN • 30–50 MINUTES

WARM-UP ACTIVITIES   3–4 minutes

(1) Stay in the big square I have marked with cones. Show me your idea of the differences between jogging and running. Keep doing about 10 seconds of each. Go!
(2) Well done. I liked the easy, small-steps jogging with arms and heels carried down low, contrasting with the longer strides and livelier, quicker running with heels, knees and arms carried much higher. All have a practice. Keep going with about 10 seconds of each. Go!

TIMED PART LAP OF 150 METRES   4–5 minutes

I will use three runs, to let you all have an easy subtraction of starting time from finishing time. Group one, zero seconds, go! Group two, ten seconds, go! (After both groups are back, groups three and four go off and are timed. Finally, group five has its run.)

GROUP ACTIVITIES   20–35 minutes

(1) Timed 50-metre sprint. Time taken for five of team to come through is taken by the sixth member of the team. Two or three attempts may be made with a different timekeeper each time. The best team time will be recorded.
(2) Standing long jump from a line. Measurement is by reference to the 2-metre sticks placed parallel with line of jump. Each takes turn at jumping, being told distance, telling someone else their distance. All best jumps are added together.
(3) Bean bag put. Each has four puts with best one marked and measured by partner. Hand must come forward from neck in put. Any backward hand movement is a throw and not allowed.
(4) Non-scoring practice at high jump stands with elastic 'bar' at a height all can clear with a scissors jump after a 3-count run up.
(5) Large-ball throw for distance marked and measured by partner. Each has three throws, using two hands with long, straight arms starting above and behind head. To help balance and throw, one foot is placed in front of the other.

TEAM SHUTTLE RELAYS; 30 metres   3–6 minutes

      X5 X3 X1 | | X2 X4 X6
1 races to give baton to 2, right hand to right hand, and stays at the end of 2's line. 2 races to pass baton to 3 and stays at the end of that line. All run one way, then back to starting side, which brings baton back to 1 to end the race.

Teacher calls out results, first to fifth, and times the winner as a target to beat in the second race. Right hand to right hand is to prevent anyone being speared in the stomach by a fumbled baton.

Team Number _____

First place in activity gains five points for a team. Fifth place gains one point.

Event	Individual Results						Combined Result	Place 1st–5th	Points 5–1
	1	2	3	4	5	6			
150 m									
50 m									
Bean bag put									
Standing long jump									
Large ball throw									
Shuttle relay									
								Total Points	
								Position in Class	

LESSON PLAN • 30–50 MINUTES

WARM-UP ACTIVITES   3–4 minutes

(1) Show me your best running inside the big square marked by cones. Is your running silent, with good lift of heels and knees?
(2) Half running, now, half watching. Watchers, tell me whose running you like and why.

(3) Thank you for your helpful comments. Now, let's watch the other half and then comment on who you particularly liked and why. Go! (Comments, thanks, then all have a last practice.)

TIMED PART LAP OF 150 METRES   4–5 minutes

(1) This is 100 metres shorter than your July run, so your rhythm will be brisker. Keep to the left to run only 150 metres.
(2) I will set you off, groups one, two and three; then four and five so that we don't have the

confusion of runners coming in before some have gone off. Subtract your start time from your finish time. Group one, zero seconds, go! Group two, five seconds, go! (etc.)

CLASS ACTIVITY; Throwing a large ball   5–8 minutes

(1) Three players of each group make a triangle, 3 metres apart. Chest pass with fingers up and elbows down, aiming at partner's chest.
(2) A bigger triangle, 5 metres apart, for a longer

throw. Start with ball beside shoulder. Push arms straight towards receiving partner. Relax hands and arms on catching.

GROUP ACTIVITIES; Five groups of six   15–28 minutes

(1) As always, the class activity is to let them practise, to improve and refine the skills already performed. In their 4 metre-sided triangles, the two trios practise: A throws to B, runs to B's position, and then back to own. B passes to C, runs to C's position and then back to own. C throws to A, and so on. Triangles can challenge each other to number of passes.
(2) Scissors jump over low elastic 'bar' tied between high jump stands. By now, all should know the side from which to approach at an angle of 40 degrees, with three strides only to prevent over-speeding and slipping on grass at take-off and on landing.
(3) 50-metre timed sprint for a new school year time, and to compare it, back in class, with the

many times from the previous two years. Each group is timed, one at a time, by a member of that group.
(4) Throwing the hoop with a partner for accuracy and medium (15–20-metre) distance. Start side-on to partner with the hoop held well back and almost touching ground. Flat hoop is pulled in semi-circle, past shoulder height and released in front of head.
(5) Partner fun runs across 30 metres: (a) Three-legged race. Side by side, hands behind back, left hand in left hand, right hand in right hand. (b) Quick walking, one to line and back, partner to line and back. (c) Sprints, there and back. (d) Any fun run of their own making.

SHUTTLE RELAYS; 30 metres apart   3–5 minutes

     X5 X3 X1 | | X2 X4 X6
1 runs to pass baton to 2 and stays at back of line. 2 runs to pass to 3 and stays at back of line. All run and stay, there and back, to finish in their

own starting positions. All carry and receive baton with right hand. Teacher calls out results and times the two races.

LESSON NOTES • 3 LESSONS DEVELOPMENT

The lesson's main emphases include

(a) A start of year, re-establishment of good traditions and habits of sensible, safe practice and wholehearted participation.

(b) Continuing to develop and refine the basic techniques in running, jumping and throwing.

Equipment needed

- 10 large balls
- 5 batons
- 3 hoops
- stopwatch
- high jump stands and elastic 'bar'
- cones for marking areas

Warm-up activities

(1) There is an impression of 'lift' in good running with heels, knees, arms, head and shoulders affected.

(2) We learn from, and remember what we see, inspired and helped by excellent demonstrations and friendly helpful comments.

(3) Class practice always follows a demonstration to use good things seen and commented on.

Timed part lap

(1) The rhythm should be between brisk and very brisk for this shortish run.

(2) Interest in results is helped by the teacher calling 'Eighteen and nineteen and twenty and twenty-one....' as they finish, so that they can subtract starting times from finishing times. (The 'and' being 0.5 seconds, to give a more accurate time.)

Class activity

(1) Throwing a larger ball at the start of the autumn term with its netball, basketball and other small-sided games, is a good way to merge athletics and games.

(2) 'Hands high with elbows down, fingers at sides of ball, thumbs towards back of ball' needs to be taught if they hold hands low.

Group activities

(1) 'Throw, follow throw to catcher and run back' practices keep them on their toes to be back, ready, before the ball comes to them again. Trios can race each other to 'make 12 passes'.

(2) A lively, springy-stepped jumper can spring a good height off a 3-count run, but will not be off balance and fall on landing as he or she might after lots of high-speed approach strides.

(3) A reminder is needed to explain how to start, judge and time each runner, so that times are consistently achieved. Each member of team starts ('Set...go!') and times one runner, then gives the runner his or her time, before going to take their own turn.

(4) This popular activity, done like a discus throw, starts with drive of rear leg, then strong turn of shoulders and upper body, then the pulling, whirling arm action right around to the front and aim and throw. A flat horizontal flight lands and stays put. A vertical flight will land and roll.

(5) In the three-legged race, on 'Set!' partners lift inside feet. On 'Go!' they step down on inside foot and run, balanced, two near, then two outer feet. Pairs take turns at starting the races and all can be challenged 'Can you invent a good, fun, partners race?'

Shuttle relays

After two years of athletic activities lessons, they should all know the pattern of a shuttle relay with its 'there and back' double run that brings them all back to their starting positions. The two or three races should be judged and timed. They might need reminding to carry and receive the baton in the right hand to avoid being speared by it.

Year 5 • April • Field Lesson 2

LESSON PLAN • 30–50 MINUTES

WARM-UP ACTIVITIES   3–4 minutes

(1) Follow the leader, 3 metres apart. Walk to first marker at 15 metres; jog to second marker at 30 metres; then run at three-quarter speed, right past third marker at 45 metres, emphasising a good heel and knee lift to reach well forward into next step.
(2) New leader for return walk, jog and run, emphasising 'straight ahead' running, with feet, arms, shoulders and head travelling straight, with no twisting, off-line deviations. (Repeat both.)

TIMED PART LAP OF 150 METRES   4–5 minutes

(1) Run this at the three-quarter speed you have just practised. Do not go off at full speed.
(2) Groups one, two and three will go off at 5 second intervals. When they are all back, groups four and five will be timed. All of you, remember to subtract your start time from your finish time. Group one, zero seconds, go! Group two, five seconds, go! Group three, ten seconds, go!

CLASS ACTIVITY; Hop, step and jump   5–8 minutes

(1) All come inside the track, facing the inside line of the straight. Take a few easy running steps up to the line and find out which is your hopping foot. It will not be a long hop.
(2) As you walk back to the same starting place within the track, can you walk into a hop, then a step. That is, one foot to same foot to opposite foot. Hop and step about the same length.
(3) Easy run up to line again, and try a hop and a bounding step.
(4) Try a hop, step and jump whose rhythm has roughly equal parts – not a huge hop, a tiny step and a poor little jump.

GROUP ACTIVITIES; Five groups of six   15–28 minutes

(1) Triple jump. Start inside the straight of the track, about 4 metres from the line. Do an easy run up to the line, then try to hop across two lanes, step across two lanes and jump across two lanes – or whatever is an easy, comfortable, safe width for you.
(2) Tennis-ball throw with a partner. Thrower stands side-on to partner with arm well back. Arm bends high over shoulder, then stretches into throw. Partner marks where ball lands with cone.
(3) Hurdling over three sets of canes on cones in two lanes. Try to plan run up to take off with correct foot for first hurdle, then say to self 'Over, 1, 2, 3, over' as lead leg goes up and down straight over hurdle. Trailing leg lifts out to side and round and down.
(4) Scissors jump over an elastic 'bar' tied between high jump stands. Start three stride lengths away from the bar, at an angle to it. Rise up on toes; step on to jumping foot; step on to other foot; then step on to jumping foot and jump. A bouncy approach.
(5) Relay baton exchange within a 20-metre area, in pairs. First runner has a 10-metre approach, and 10 metres beyond take-over box. Pairs practise the exchange, left hand to inverted V of right hand, running, trying to make exchange at 10–12 metres.

LONG LINE, END TO END RELAY   3–5 minutes

Line 1 | X1 X2 X3 X4 X5 X6 | Line 2
1 races to touch Line 1; runs past team to touch Line 2; runs back to give baton to 2, who repeats it all. Each team member repeats this sequence and relay ends with baton passed from 6 back to 1.

LESSON NOTES • 3 LESSONS DEVELOPMENT

The lesson's main emphases include

(a) Enjoyment of the variety – running, relays, throwing and jumping.
(b) Making simple judgements about their own and others' performances and using this information to improve the quality of their own performance.

Equipment needed

- 9 tennis balls
- 5 batons
- 6 canes on 12 cones to make hurdles
- high jump stands and elastic 'bar'
- marker cones

Warm-up activities

(1) You mirror your leader's good quality running with its emphasis on lifting knees and thighs.
(2) You mirror your partner's straightness, particularly in arm action and placement of feet. Running on the straight line helps.

Timed part lap

(1) 'Three-quarter speed' running means leaving something in reserve; 'coasting', not sprinting. Still pursue good quality, efficient running, because that is least tiring.
(2) Teacher lines them up at start, then moves to finish line from which to shout starting instructions and give finishing times.

Class activity

(1) Explain 'A hop is where you take off and land on the same foot'. Right to right or left to left.
(2) Hop and step is right to right to left, or left to left to right. Try for a hop and a step of roughly equal parts, not the often-seen long ho-o-op followed by a tiny step.
(3) Feel the stepping leg reaching up and ahead for a good step.
(4) Demonstrate with good performers showing 'One and two and three'.

Group activities

(1) Because we are performing on grass, the whole triple jump must be carefully practised at half speed, avoiding any unpleasant impact on knee and ankle joints.
(2) Each thrower has three throws, then changes places. Lines with a number or a tape parallel to throws can give the distances.
(3) From the start line they aim to adjust to have correct take-off foot leading over first hurdle, coming straight down quickly to continue speeding up to and over next hurdle. Distances between hurdles can be different in two lanes to accommodate different speeds and leg lengths.
(4) Remind jumpers that they do not need to keep coming back to same starting side. They can turn around at landing side, take three steps back, approach again along line of previous jump and jump at same angle to bar again. Slow approach and soft landing.
(5) It is important that both runners know that change-over is not wanted or expected until the receiver has run 10–12 metres – he or she can judge it nicely by saying 'Running, running, reaching, taking' which takes up about 10 metres of the box.

Long line, end to end, relay

Five leaders with batons in left hand race to touch line with a foot and turn to race past right side of own team to touch other end line. They turn and race back to give baton to right hand of gently moving second runner on right side of team. Teacher times and judges the two or three popular and exciting races.

LESSON PLAN • 30–50 MINUTES

WARM-UP ACTIVITIES   3–4 minutes

(1) Lines of six quick walk behind a leader. End person jogs up to front to become new leader, then next end person does the same.
(2) Lines now jog behind leader. End person sprints to front of line, followed by next end person, and so on.
(3) Race, among groups, doing the two activities above, and finishing standing still behind original leader.

TIMED LAP OR PART LAP OF 200 METRES   4–5 minutes

(1) Run on left of track as near to the inside line as possible to avoid adding to the distance. Keeping a steady, medium-speed rhythm is better than running too fast at the start and then fading.
(2) Groups will go off at 5 second intervals, listening carefully for starting and finishing times to let you work out your time. Group one, zero seconds, go! Group two, five seconds, go! (etc.)

CLASS ACTIVITY; Relay baton exchange   5–8 minutes

(1) 2 has a take-over area of 20 metres marked with cones. 2, look behind you for a mark on the ground at 4–5 metres. Start running when your partner reaches the mark.
(2) 1, run in fast and hand over, well into the box, after 10–12 metres. Ready? Go!
(3) Repeat the practice, and adjust where necessary, to try to improve the speed and place of take-over, then change duties.

GROUP ACTIVITIES; Five groups of six   15–28 minutes

(1) Running, relay take-over practices within 20-metre marked area. Pairs race each other one way, rest a few seconds, then race back in opposite direction. Take-over box applies both ways.
(2) Throwing hoop for distance with partner. Thrower starts side-on to direction of throw. Hoop is held low and well back, horizontal with fingers above and thumb below. Straight arm pulls around at shoulder height in a semi-circle, releasing hoop at head height.
(3) 50-metre timed sprint. Each takes turn at starting and timing another member of the group.
Timekeeper tells runner the result. Runners start, semi-crouched, one foot forward, arms bent.
(4) Putting the bean bag. Partner marks best of three puts. Stand side-on, weight well back over rear foot, bean bag tight into neck. Arms must not go back from neck into put.
(5) Partners standing long jump across width of track. 1 does a standing long jump and stands still. 2 starts in line with 1's landing and does standing long jump. They count how many jumps are needed to cross track, competing with other couples.

THREES, THERE-AND-BACK RELAY   3–5 minutes

X1 |	X2 |	X3 |	|
X4 |	X5 |	X6 |	|

Each group has two trios with each member at a line. 1 and 4 race to give baton to 2 and 5 who race to pass it on to 3 and 6 who race to end line, turn and race to give baton back to previous runner, and so on, back to starting runners, 1 and 4, who race past starting line to finish.

LESSON NOTES • 3 LESSONS DEVELOPMENT

The lesson's main emphases include

(a) Being praised for responding immediately, moving from place to place and activity to activity quickly, thus enabling all parts of the lesson to be successfully achieved.

(b) Demonstrating positive attitudes to participation in vigorous physical activity.

Equipment needed

- 15 batons
- 9 bean bags
- 3 hoops
- stopwatch
- marker cones for relays and throws
- measuring tape

Warm-up activities

(1) Leaders give teams good space by avoiding others in the designated area. A jog is quick enough to overtake quick walkers. Only one at a time overtakes.

(2) It now needs a sprint to overtake five joggers.

(3) On 'Go!' teams have to complete each of two overtaking practices. 'Only one may overtake at a time' must be emphasised.

Timed lap or part lap

(1) Run tall and relaxed with no tension in hands or arms. Let legs reach well forward by lifting heels and knees. Even 10 cm on each step will speed you up.

(2) When timing them at the end of the run, the teacher calls out '32 and 33 and 34 and 35' with the 'and' being 0.5 seconds. This gives a more accurate time as they subtract starting time from finishing time.

Class activity

(1) Long line of 1s start on inside line of straight of track. 2s at start of marked take-over will be in a line down the centre of the field. Most primary school relay runners do not run far enough before receiving baton at speed. They need to practise starting as the incoming runner passes a check mark on the ground.

Group activities

(1) The relay can move on to the track for races among three couples. Demonstrate with excellent pairs, taking baton at speed.

(2) Distance lines which are used for large ball throws serve for hoops also. If a tape is placed parallel to the line of throws, the partner who marks where the hoop lands (not rolls to) can give an accurate distance to throwing partner, then change over.

(3) Sprinter should be crouched for start, one foot and arm forward, weight forward, to respond explosively to 'Go!' He or she should be told to 'Race past timekeeper before slowing'.

(4) From a standing, side-on, start position with feet wide apart, the rear leg drives you forward, still side-on. Then the upper body and shoulders rotate to face forward. Next, the hand comes forward from the neck (back is a throw and not allowed) and the arm stretches forward at an angle of about 60 degrees. The final action is a snap of the wrist into the high follow through.

(5) In a standing long jump, feet are slightly apart. Knees bend and arms swing down behind you. Legs drive up and forward and arms reach forward, helping the action. Knees bend to land to take feet as far forward as possible.

Threes, there-and-back relay

Easy to organise if four cones mark the lines and each member is numbered one, two, three. The teacher stands beside first runner, starts the race, judges and times it. Two or three races should produce improved times.

LESSON PLAN • 30–50 MINUTES

WARM-UP ACTIVITIES   3–4 minutes

(1) Walk to the first cone at 15 metres. Jog to the second cone at 30 metres. Run quickly from second to third cone at 45 metres counting the number of sprinting strides to take you to third cone.

(2) Turn around and repeat back to starting line. This time, lift heels and knees to help you lengthen each stride and see if you need fewer strides for the 15-metre sprint.

TIMED LAP OF 250 METRES   4–5 minutes

(1) No-one is chasing you around the track; it's not a race. It is a measurement of your ability to run the distance calmly and comfortably, without finishing up feeling shattered.

(2) Keep to the left on the track. Do not run wide or you add extra metres. Groups will go off at 5 second intervals. Group one, zero seconds, go! Group two, five seconds, go! (etc.)

CLASS ACTIVITY; Tennis ball throw   5–8 minutes

(1) We have always thrown from a standing position. Today, we will add a couple of steps to give you a bit more power. All practise the action without the ball. Stand side-on with throwing arm back. Step rear foot across front foot. Long step to side with front foot still side-on, leaning well back over rear foot.
(2) Drive with rear leg; pull shoulders around to front and let throwing arm bend to come over the shoulder and straighten into throw. It becomes: step, step, leg, body, arm. Practise without a ball.
(3) At about 20 metres apart, carefully practise the two steps into your throw. Forward arm bends up in front to balance you.

GROUP ACTIVITIES; Five groups of six   15–28 minutes

(1) Stepping into tennis-ball throw for distance. More power can be added by jumping off from one foot into your 'Side-on, step, step, throw'. Jump from the opposite foot to the throwing arm.
(2) Hurdling over three sets of hurdles made from canes on cones. Adjust your crouch start position so that you reach and clear the first hurdle with the correct leading leg. It might mean changing your usual way of starting, by making your front foot become the back one.
(3) Scissors high jump over elastic 'bar' tied between high jump stands. Use a 3-step or a slow, careful, 5-step approach, starting the run-up with the same foot that you jump with.
(4) Throwing large ball with a 2-step approach. Start with the ball held above and behind head with straight arms. Take one step forward, leaning back. Take a second step forward, leaning back and throw with feeling of weight moving forward into vigorous throw. Partner marks best of three landing places of ball.
(5) 75-metre timed sprint. Each member of the group is timed and then takes a turn at starting and timekeeping another runner.

ROUND AND ROUND THE TRACK, ONE MINUTE RELAY   3–5 minutes

Teams space out at the six marked starting places which divide the track equally into sixths of a lap. They race and continue around the track for one minute at which point the teacher blows a whistle as a signal for all to stop. The team that has run the furthest at the whistle is the winner. For example, 'Well done, team two, just over two laps and thirteen change-overs of the baton'.

LESSON NOTES • 3 LESSONS DEVELOPMENT

The lesson's main emphases include

(a) Taking part wholeheartedly in activities that develop health, strength and endurance.

(b) Feeling and looking better, thanks to vigorous participation in these very physical lessons.

Equipment needed

- 15 tennis balls
- 9 large balls
- 5 batons
- measuring tape
- stopwatch
- 6 canes on 12 cones to make hurdles
- high jump stands and elastic 'bar'
- marker cones for warm-ups, throws, relays

Warm-up activities

(1) Counting the sprinting strides is easier if they count the number of strikes by the foot that hits the line at the start of the sprint, then double the number.

(2) Stride length is increased by a greater lift of knees and thighs. If stride speed remains the same while increasing stride length, the running must be quicker.

Timed lap or part lap

(1) We want them to be pleased with their ability to complete the distance at a reasonable rhythm. And we want them to look and feel fitter, month by month.

(2) As always, they subtract start times from finish times to be recorded and, maybe, admired back in class later.

Class activity

(1) Unrestrained, they will take lots of running steps as a preamble to throwing. They will do as well taking only the two steps, moving into the side-on, throwing position.

(2) Like any thrower (of javelin, discus, hoop, for example) the rear leg drive, the rotation of upper body, and the pulling action into the throw all combine to produce maximum forward speed of object.

(3) 'One (cross step), two (side step), three (the throw)' is the rhythm. Good performers can be used to demonstrate the technique.

Group activities

(1) Start with feet together, facing forward. Jump into first, cross-over step by a push from the opposite foot to the throwing side. This spring up and turn, with hand going back, and body leaning back transfers the body weight forward strongly into the last step and throw.

(2) Keep the distance to the first hurdle consistent at 10 metres to let them repeat the run-in to clear the first hurdle from the same sprint start position each time, knowing which foot is forward and which is back. Three steps are taken between the hurdles as they think or say 'Over, 1, 2, 3, over, 1, 2, 3, over'.

(3) If a 5-step approach is used from grass to grass take-off, it must be slow and bouncy and completely under control to give a safe, easy landing after clearing the low 'bar'.

(4) Once again, if unrestrained, they will run a long way as a build-up to throwing. A 2-step approach, with strong backward bend (not possible if running) and forceful long arm throw combine to give very good results.

(5) They will have one timed run each for maximum effort.

Round and round the track, one minute relay

Encourage runners to 'Keep to the left of the track on the bends, than go back to your own position for the take-over' to lessen wide side running on outer arc of track. They should also try to 'Keep baton moving throughout by taking it, running'.

LESSON PLAN • 30–50 MINUTES

WARM-UP ACTIVITIES   3–4 minutes

(1) Jog side by side with a partner, with one of you setting the rhythm, and showing how you ran during the previous lesson's 250-metre jog/run. I will call out 'Walk!' after 15 seconds. Go!
(2) Now the other partner shows a good 250-metre lap rhythm and speed. Once again I will call out 'Walk!' after 15 seconds. Go!
(3) Now you will each have another practice at your estimated jog or run speed, for 15 seconds. I will call 'Change!' for the second leader to go straight into his or her lap rhythm.

TIMED LAP OR PART LAP OF 250 METRES   4–5 minutes

(1) I hope you can now feel a good, steady rhythm that you can maintain without becoming too shattered. If in doubt, slow down. Keep left to run only 250 metres, not wide and more.
(2) Let's reverse the order this month. Group five, zero seconds, go! Group four, five seconds, go! (etc.)

CLASS ACTIVITY; Throwing a hoop   5–8 minutes

(1) 1s, stand astride the throwing line (inside line of track) with hoop held well back, resting on ground. Fingers are over, thumb under, and hoop is held almost horizontal, not pointing up.
(2) Without letting go, pull it from straight behind you to straight in front of you with a long, straight arm pull, all at about shoulder height. Take it back again, still with straight arm.
(3) Now the whole movement, letting go carefully as you aim to land it by your partner, 15 metres away. Make it fly flat.

GROUP ACTIVITIES; Five groups of six   15–28 minutes

(1) Throwing hoop for accuracy and medium distance. They practise forward and backward rotation without releasing it, and feel the rear leg drive, the upper body rotation, and the aim and release. Practise, then make it fly horizontally to land and settle, not land on edge and roll.
(2) Pairs, racing over three hurdles after a 10-metre run-in, and with three steps in between – over, 1, 2, 3, over – with same foot leading every time. Pairs race to finish 10 metres past last hurdle.
(3) Measured tennis-ball throw after a 2-step approach to take you up to the throwing line. Partner marks and measures best of three.
(4) Relay baton exchange within 20-metre box on track. Partners race other couples to a point 10 metres beyond take-over zone, turn around, rest for a few moments, then race back to start line in reverse order, saying 'Running, running, reaching, taking' to co-ordinate.
(5) Partner fun runs, there and back across 20 metres, with each pair having turns at starting: (a) quick walk; (b) sprint; (c) skipping; (d) three-legged race; (e) invent a simple, partner fun run.

AROUND THE TRACK RELAYS   3–5 minutes

With team five on the inside and team one on the outside, each team member has a starting place next to a marker on the track. A one-lap race with receivers taking batons on the move in the right hand with inverted V of thumb and first finger presenting a target for the incoming runner with baton in left hand. In next race teams reverse starting positions. Teacher calls out results and times, and praises smooth, neat, co-ordinated, running take-overs of baton.

LESSON NOTES • 3 LESSONS DEVELOPMENT

The lesson's main emphases include

(a) End of year praise for their co-operation which enabled these lessons to be successfully carried out.

(b) Demonstrating skilful performances and the ability to repeat them.

Equipment needed

- 15 hoops
- 9 tennis balls
- 6 skipping ropes
- 5 batons
- marker cones
- measuring tape
- 6 canes on 12 cones to make hurdles

Warm-up activities

(1) After three years of athletics experiences they should be able to perform at a sensible, one-lap speed.

(2) Going too fast will be the main fault. Partner should slow them down a bit in pursuit of something they can perform continuously.

(3) They should be able to reproduce their practised, estimated lap speed in the actual lap run.

Timed lap or part lap

(1) They can be asked to run easily on the spot at what they estimate to be an appropriate speed. The teacher can comment on any wildly over-speed running and demonstrate an example of good running for 250 metres.

(2) 1s usually start first, with least time to get their breath back after the warm-up. Here, they are having a different start time and a better 'breather' first.

Class activity

(1) Teacher checks starting positions of hoops and grips in this 'ready' position.
(2) The pull forward and back is similar to the wind up by a discus thrower, feeling the weight transferring forward and back, ready.

(3) Aiming at about 60 degrees gives a good flight of the hoop which should be kept horizontal in flight, like a discus. Practice is then repeated with number two.

Group activities

(1) Throw for control and accuracy first until the knack of throwing is learned. Then challenge them to throw it 20 metres to land beautifully flat on the grass straight ahead of thrower.
(2) The previous month's adjustment of starting position of feet should be remembered. Leading leg goes straight up and down over hurdle. Trailing leg lifts up and around to one side to avoid crashing into the hurdle.
(3) Insist on a 2-step approach, only, as preparation for the turn to side-on throw. Most do not aim high enough to 'let the ball see a long way ahead.'
(4) Receiver should not put hand back until well into the running action. Giver should not try to pass the baton until a point about 10-12 metres inside area. Most primary school take-overs occur far too anxiously early, long before the baton has got speed up.
(5) Fun runners can be challenged 'Can anyone invent a simple fun run race? How about a different action – hopping or bouncing?'

Around the track relays

Relays are easily the most popular and memorable part of the lesson, and must never be missed out. It is important to provide fairness by changing the order so that the same team is not always on the outside of the track, running further than anyone else. Timing winners and calling out all results is equally important.

Year 5 • Team Competition Lesson on Field

LESSON PLAN • 30–50 MINUTES

WARM-UP ACTIVITIES
3–4 minutes

(1) Side by side with a partner, can you keep together at the same easy jogging speed? Try to 'feel' the repeating rhythm of your jogging as you keep in unison, left, right, left, right, together.
(2) Walking, side by side now. When ready, change to easy, half speed running with more lift in heels and knees than in your jogging.
(3) Finally, see how well you keep together in walking, then jogging, then running, then walking, giving about 10 seconds to each.

TIMED PART LAP OF 200 METRES
4–5 minutes

This is a timed team activity. Aim to finish, still running, by performing at a sensible, manageable pace. Do not go off too fast and then finish walking in, adding lots of seconds to your team's score. Remember, also, to subtract your start time from your finish time. Groups will go off at 5 second intervals.

GROUP ACTIVITIES; Five groups of six
20–35 minutes

(1) Timed 60-metre sprint. Each team member is timed individually by another team member. Before rotating groups, the teacher checks time taken by whole team to do the distance.
(2) Throwing the hoop. Partners mark best of three throws and check distance on tape at side of area. Result only counts if it lands within permitted, fairly narrow sector. Straight is best because very wide is disqualified and quite wide diminishes distance.
(3) Non-scoring hurdling over five sets of canes on pairs of cones. Run to first hurdle is 10 metres. Distance between hurdles is 4–5 metres. Run to finish line is 10 metres. On the way back for next hurdles practice, they can try easy triple jump practice after a short run. Three, almost equal parts, hop, step, jump – not the usual huge hop, little step, very poor jump.
(4) Trios, three standing long jumps each. Two trios within the group work on either side of measuring tape. 1 starts at the line and does three jumps, each from a standing start. 2 starts beside 1's line of toes after three jumps, and does a set of three jumps. 3 jumps from 2's landing place. Trio result is measured and marked as a challenge to other groups.
(5) Tennis-ball throw, allowing a 2-step approach to throwing line. Partner judges, marks and gives measurement of best of three throws. Same tape can serve to measure both hoop throw and tennis-ball throw if placed on ground between them.

TEAM SHUTTLE RELAYS; 30 metres
3–6 minutes

    X5 X3 X1 I   I X2 X4 X6

1 races to hand baton to 2 and stays at end of 2's line. 2 races to give baton to 3 and stays at the back of 3's line. Each has two runs, to opposite side, then back to own side. Race ends with 5 giving baton back to 1. Baton is carried and received in right hand. Teacher calls out results, first to fifth, and times winning team.

Team Number _____

First place in activity gains five points for a team. Fifth place gains one point.

Event	Individual Results						Combined Result	Place 1st–5th	Points 5–1
	1	2	3	4	5	6			
200 m									
75 m									
Hoop throw									
Team long jump									
Tennis ball throw									
Shuttle relay									
								Total Points	
								Position in Class	

LESSON PLAN • 30–50 MINUTES

WARM-UP ACTIVITIES   3–4 minutes

(1) Run and jump high and run and jump long over the lines of the track. Remind yourself which foot you push off with in the two kinds of jumps. It's not always the same one.

(2) Now run along a line to check out how good your 'straight ahead' running is. Arms, feet, head and shoulders should all be steady, pointing straight ahead, with no side to side wobbling.

TIMED PART LAP OF 100 METRES   3–5 minutes

(1) This is a speedy run all the way. Plan a relaxed, steady, three-quarter speed you can keep up to the end. Keep hands, arms and legs relaxed to avoid any tension or tightness.

(2) Groups one, two and three will go off first at five second intervals. Then, groups four and five will go off. Remember to subtract your starting time from your finishing time.

CLASS ACTIVITY; Throwing large ball   5–8 minutes

(1) Trios, in a triangle formation, practise 'Pass and follow'. A passes to B and runs the 5 metres to B's place. B passes to C and runs to C's place. C runs, carrying the ball to what was A's place, and the practice starts all over again
(2) Trios can compete to make six sets of complete triangles.

GROUP ACTIVITIES; Five groups of six   16–28 minutes

(1) Large-ball throw in lines of three, about 7–10 metres apart. Longish, accurate throwing is practised as 1 throws to 2, 2 throws to 3, 3 throws to 2, 2 throws it back to 1. Throw is with both hands from above and behind head, and two steps into the throw with one foot in front of the other are allowed. Trios sensibly stand at a manageable distance apart for an easy, high catch.
(2) 50-metre timed sprint, individually timed by one of group. A new school year reminder of how to start race (Set…go!) and how to operate and read the stopwatch is recommended.
(3) Standing high jump and 3-step approach scissors jump with a partner holding a cane low. Jump can be from facing cane at arms length, or from standing side-on. Scissors jump has a 45-degree angle approach and can be done from both sides along same diagonal line.
(4) Bean bag putting with a partner, using width of track to put across. One bag can be used, from side to side. Putter stands side-on to line of put with bean bag against neck, elbow high behind. Forward arm is bent and high to balance you. Leg drive forward, upper body rotation to front, then explosive push of arm forward from neck.
(5) Shuttle relay practices and races; two teams of three across 30 metres. Baton starts at front of line with two runners. 1 runs to pass to 2 and stays at the back of 2's line. 2 runs to give baton to 3 and stays at back of 3's line. 3 races to give baton to 1, and so on until all are back to starting places.

SHUTTLE RELAYS; 30 metres (as above)   3–5 minutes

        X5 X3 X1 | | X2 X4 X6   races.
Teacher call out results and times winners of two

LESSON NOTES • 3 LESSONS DEVELOPMENT

The lesson's main emphases include

(a) Re-establishing the habit of good listening and responding, and wholehearted participation by an age group with enormous potential for high quality physical education performances.

(b) Working hard to develop and improve the basic techniques of running and relays, jumping and throwing.

Equipment needed

- 5 batons
- 3 bean bags
- 3 canes
- 2 large balls
- stopwatch
- marker cones for relays and throws

Warm-up activities

(1) Using lines on track gives practice in adjusting run-ups for both high and long jumps. Medium jumps only since they are landing on grass.
(2) Waves of runners, one to each line, are sent down track. On return run along same lines, the teacher can see and then demonstrate with excellent performers. 'Watch their straight ahead everything – head, shoulders, arms and legs. Very efficient!'.

Timed part lap

(1) Each of the five, Year 6 lessons will feature a different length, timed part lap or lap for variety and to give them all known, final year times to take to their next school.

Class activity

(1) A combination of throwing for accuracy and running for speed. Dome shaped cones can be used to make triangle.

(2) Style of passing will be relevant to netball, basketball or rugby in September's games lessons.

Group activities

(1)   X1   X2   X3
Large-ball throw from 1 to 2 to 3 and back to 2 to 1, is practised first, and then can be made competitive against the other trio in your group.
(2) Runners start in a crouched, sprint start position, one foot and opposite arm bent forward, with weight inclined forward, ready. They are told to 'Finish fast, right past your timekeeper'.
(3) After six, standing high jumps each, they change to the gentle running, 3-step scissors jump. Dynamic, strong-legged, eleven-year olds will surprise themselves and the teacher with their high clearances of the low cane in both styles of jump.

(4) In the side-on, feet wide astride, starting position, they can have two or three preparatory rocks back and forward, as shot putters do, before their explosive body turn and arm extension forward. The bean bag must never come away from the neck backwards; this is deemed to be a throw and is not allowed.
(5) The main feature of the shuttle relay is that you carry and pass with the right hand. This prevents the baton spearing someone as can happen if you have to reach across their body to their opposite left hand. They must be stationary for change-over at the line.

Team shuttle relays

The relay is the most exciting and memorable part of the lesson for the pupils and must never be omitted. If, for some reason, the lesson is cut short, some other, earlier part must be sacrificed to leave time, ideally, for at least two relays. The teacher stands at the start/finish line, calls out all the results and times the winner to give all groups something to try to beat in the second race.

Year 6 • April • Field Lesson 2

LESSON PLAN • 30–50 MINUTES

WARM-UP ACTIVITIES   3–4 minutes

(1) Jog to marker at 25 metres. Walk to marker at 50 metres. Jog to marker at 75 metres. Turn around, ready to come back again.

(2) For about 25 seconds, practise running at a sensible speed that you think you can keep up for your 150-metre timed lap.

TIMED PART LAP OF 150 METRES   4–5 minutes

(1) I hope this is more of a run and less of a jog as we come to the end of Year 6. However, run in such a sensible way that you finish feeling fit for the rest of the lesson.

(2) Keep well to the left of the track to avoid adding distance to the 150 metres. Group one, zero seconds, go! Group two, five seconds, go! (etc.)

CLASS ACTIVITY; Scaled down long jump   5–8 minutes

(1) We will do a careful, safe practice of long jump. Pretend inside line of the track is the take-off board. Stand on the line with your back to the track. Start with feet together, then run away from the track. Build up to half speed for a long jump. Stop and mark the spot where you would have taken off.

(2) Stand with feet together on your mark. Run up to track at half speed, and see if you hit the line with your take-off foot for a very careful long jump, landing with feet together.
(3) Practise carefully from your mark, landing well controlled each time, after feeling the leading leg reach well forward.

GROUP ACTIVITIES; Five groups of six   15–28 minutes

(1) Long jumping. Partner watches your restrained run and jump to see how near your take-off foot was to line, from the marked starting point about 10 metres back. Look for front leg reaching forward and rear leg catching up for landing.
(2) Tennis-ball throw after 2-step approach. Side on, step right foot across left, taking arm well back. Left foot steps wide to side. Rear leg drives forward, upper body rotates to front, throwing arm bends to come high over shoulder into throw.
(3) Hurdling over three sets of canes on pairs of cones. After 10-metre approach, they lead with correct foot over first hurdle, then three strides in between. 'Over, 1, 2, 3, over'. They walk back on leading leg side of hurdles, lifting trailing leg up and round.
(4) Throwing hoop to partner at 15-20 metres. Partner watches for and coaches: (a) wide, side-on stance, hoop held just under horizontal, well back in straight arm, fingers over, thumb under; (b) two or three discus style forward and backward, preparatory rotations with arm at shoulder height; (c) throw, preceded by rear leg drive, rotation of upper body and straight arm pulling action.
(5) 60-metre timed sprint, with each team member being individually timed by another team member. One run only, emphasising 'Run straight, lifting heels and knees for good strides'.

PARTNERS, SIDE LINES TOUCH RELAYS   3–5 minutes

Partners stand, side by side, down centre area of field, at equal distances from inside lines of track. On 'Go!' one races to touch nearer side line, turns, races back to touch hand of partner who does same to own nearer line. Teacher calls out results as pairs finish together. One or two more races should be started and judged.

LESSON NOTES • 3 LESSONS DEVELOPMENT

The lesson's main emphases include

(a) Appreciating how much a partner's co-operation contributes to our learning.

(b) Being physically active, engaging in activities that develop health, strength and fitness.

Equipment needed

- 9 tennis balls
- 3 hoops
- 6 canes on 12 cones to make hurdles
- cones as markers for warm-up and throws
- stopwatch

Warm-up activities

(1) Jogging is easy running with low arms and heels, ideally with a regular 'One, two, three, four' rhythm.

(2) For the lap speed practice the arms and heels will come higher, and there will be more forward incline of body, as you reach forward with your strides.

Timed lap or part lap

(1) Guidance by the observant teacher will have helped them to practise running short bursts at sensible 150-metre speed in the warm-up.

(2) An exact metre wheel reading of outside lane will tell them how many extra metres running wide entails.

Class activity

(1) Assuming no sand for landing in, this practice has to be 'scaled down' for safety, but the learning of the technique can still go ahead. Emphasise that it does not take many strides to reach a satisfactory speed for a long jump take-off.

(2) It helps if you start with the eventual take-off foot.

(3) The 'mark' guide on the track can be a small stone, weed, long piece of grass, bare patch, or a light or dark area.

Group activities

(1) We are long jumping for style and controlled run-up, not length. The result will be about half of what they would do with a proper landing area, but their understanding of the main features can be gained – short run up enough, both legs reaching forward.

(2) Partner marks best of three throws, judging to where ball lands, not where it rolls. A jumping turn into the first of the two, side-on steps, gives good transfer forward into throw.

(3) Keeping a consistent, 10-metre approach to first hurdle, every lesson, enables them to use a sprint start position of feet that brings them to clear the first hurdle correctly every time. Doing this correctly and at speed also gives them the momentum to do three in-between strides easily.

(4) The hoop throw is for accuracy as much as for distance. The release should be with a straight arm from just in front of your head, releasing at about 60 degrees. Aim to make it fly flat so that it lands and settles, without rolling.

(5) When it was only a 50-metre timed sprint, they often had a second timed run. Here, do one only, running right past the timekeeper with no slowing down at the line – a common fault.

Partners, side lines touch relay

If the second partner runs from a standing start in the first race, and then a running start in the second race, the greatly improved times being called out by the teacher will show the class the importance of a running baton change-over in relays.

LESSON PLAN • 30–50 MINUTES

WARM-UP ACTIVITIES   3–4 minutes

(1) Follow the leader where first leader is challenged to 'Show your partner three athletic skills that you have enjoyed in your four-year programme, always keeping on the move'. He or she will choose from jogging, running, long jumping, high jumping, hurdling or triple jumping.
(2) 'Second leader, can you join up those three athletic skills into a little sequence, maybe using jogging to link them together?'

TIMED LAP OR PART LAP OF 200 METRES   4–5 minutes

(1) Running on the spot, show me your idea of a sensible, 200-metre lap speed that you think you can keep up without distress.
(2) As always, subtract your start time from your finish time.

CLASS ACTIVITY; Relay baton take-over   5–8 minutes

(1) Baton in left hand, 1. Race to pass baton to 2, running, at about half way point in the take-over area marked with cones. 2 receives in right hand – held back and still, with inverted V of thumb and first finger the target. Go!
(2) Same order again, correcting any over-early or late starts to your running, 2. Have you found a check mark on the ground as a guide?
(3) Change order and practise twice. Then race in each direction followed by demonstrations.

GROUP ACTIVITIES; Five groups of six   15–28 minutes

(1) Relay practice on track with 20 metres take-over marked by cones. Partners practise to do transfer at about 10–12 metres, with both running fast. Partners then race other couples.
(2) Scissors high jump over elastic 'bar' tied between high jump stands at about 60 cm which is low enough for most to clear and land safely, but high enough to need the correct technique. If 'bar' is hit, it does not matter because it does not impede.
(3) Large ball throw with two hands starting above and behind head. A 2-step approach to throwing line, accompanied by a strong backward bend of upper body, provides good weight transfer forward into throw which is marked and measured by partner.
(4) Hop, step and jump, taking off from inside line of track. Aim to do an almost equal length, not too long, hop, step and jump. Even without the sand for landing, the main features – consistent take-off at line, equal length hops, steps and jumps, spreading energy over whole event, landing with feet both forward – can be learned in this scaled-down version.
(5) Partner fun runs over 25 metres. To line and back races: (a) quick walking; (b) skipping; (c) sprinting; (d) three-legged race; (e) bowl a hoop; (f) any other good ideas they have.

TO END LINES AND BACK RELAY   3–5 minutes

Line 1 | X1 X2 X3 X4 X5 X6 | Line 2
1 runs to Line 1, turns and runs past teams to Line 2, turns and races to give baton to 2 who repeats it all. Race ends with 6 giving baton to 1. Baton passes from left hand to right hand, on the move.

LESSON NOTES • 3 LESSONS DEVELOPMENT

The lesson's main emphases include

(a) Participating wholeheartedly in these physically challenging lessons in the fresh air.

(b) Recognising and following safety procedures and always being mindful of others.

Equipment needed

- 15 batons
- 6 skipping ropes
- 9 large balls
- 6 hoops
- high jump stands and elastic 'bar'
- marker cones for relays

Warm-up activities

(1) Keep about 3 metres behind leader who will jog or run as a preparation for the hurdling, triple jumping or high jumping. Follower's take-off foot may be different to partner's

(2) Sequence can be triangular – e.g. a running side, a run-and-jump side, and a hurdling side, back to starting places.

Timed lap or part lap

(1) An easy, repeating rhythm, jog/run is no more energetic than quick walking and Year 6 pupils should be able to maintain it over 200 metres.

(2) They go off in groups at 5 second intervals, listening for their starting and finishing times. 'Group one, zero seconds, go! Group two, five seconds, go!' (etc.)

Class activity

(1) They can practise across field from inside line of track to opposite inside line of track, with take-over 20 metres clearly marked as their guide for giving/receiving baton.

(2) The 'mark on the track' can be a small stone, leaf, weed, piece of long grass, bare patch, light or dark patch.

(3) 'Look at the demonstration and tell me the good points that we might learn from and copy'.

Group activities

(1) When incoming runner passes check mark on ground, outgoing runner starts running so that baton is taken on the move. Both should know that baton transfer will not be expected or attempted before about 10–12 metres of running by outgoing receiver.

(2) Elastic 'bar' does not impede the jumper in any way or hurt their shins. 'Bar' is kept low enough to deter from foolhardy, fast, high jumping that is dangerous when performing on grass. A 3-, or at most, 5-step approach run must be slowly and carefully used.

(3) The long lever of straight arms, body bending back and forward on a good wide base with one foot forward, one back, provides a powerful whip-like action in the whole body. Aim it high enough 'to let the ball see its target at about 15–20 metres'.

(4) The usual fault is a long hop using up all forward momentum, energy and speed, followed by a tiny step and a quick, short jump. If they practise, saying 'Hop…and step…and jump' with a three equal-parts rhythm, a better, overall performance is achieved.

(5) One partner races to the 25-metre line and back, touches partner who repeats it all. Pairs take turns at starting the activities fairly.

To end lines and back relay

Runner can speed team up by jumping into a crouched turn at each line for a quick re-start. Each new receiver steps out to the right. Teacher calls out all results as they finish and times winners. Second race should be faster after the first practice.

LESSON PLAN • 30–50 MINUTES

WARM-UP ACTIVITIES   3–4 minutes

(1) Stand on one foot. Lift and reach forward with the foot to touch (paw at) the ground in front of you. Now, stand on the same foot, but this time, lift other knee and thigh higher before reaching out to paw ground again. Your second reach will be longer.
(2) Walk to first marker, jog to second, and then run, emphasising a better knee and thigh lift than you normally use. Turn around and repeat back to start and I will look out for strong running with a lively lift and reach in the forward leg to show you. (Demonstrations and comment. Further practice to improve.)

TIMED LAP OF 250 METRES   4–5 minutes

(1) This is no marathon, but it is no sprint either. I just want you to prove to yourselves how fit you are by completing the run, recovering quite quickly, and feeling pleased with yourselves.
(2) Group five going off first this time. Zero seconds, go! Group four, five seconds, go! (etc.)

CLASS ACTIVITY; Bean bag put   5–8 minutes

(1) You and partner, on opposite sides of the track, side-on to each other. Feet together, hand against neck as if you had the bean bag there, elbow high to rear, weight back over rear foot.
(2) Take a short step towards partner with nearer foot. Close other foot to first foot, then take long step to side with foot nearer partner, and go into your putting action, with arm moving straight forward into vigorous put.
(3) Now try it with one bean bag, having alternate puts. Step, close, step and put, using leg drive, body rotation, before arm push.

GROUP ACTIVITIES; Five groups of six   15–28 minutes

(1) Bean bag put across track with a chasse (step, close, step) into the side-on position for the put forward from neck.
(2) Standing high, and 3-step scissors jump over low cane held by kneeling partner. Standing high can be practised from arms length, facing or side-on to cane. Partner can estimate height. '65 cm Brilliant!' For scissors jump, they use a 3-step 45-degree angle approach.
(3) 60-metre timed sprint, hoping for improved times, compared with the April times recorded in class. Do one timed run, only.
(4) Tennis-ball measured throw from a line.
Partner judges, marks and measures best of three performances. Starting back from line, they aim to spring up and forward, turning with two strides into a wide, side-on position for the throw. Rear leg drive and upper body turn precede bend of throwing arm over shoulder before stretching into aim and throw at 60 degrees.
(5) Hurdling over five sets of canes-on-cones hurdles, trying to keep up the 'Over, 1, 2, 3, over, 1, 2, 3, over'. pattern of 3-step running between hurdles. As they walk back to start, they can practise 'Hop…and step…and jump' to feel the three parts being given equal importance.

ROUND THE TRACK RELAYS   3–5 minutes

Two races around track, with six runners starting from marked positions on track. Lane positions are reversed for second race.

LESSON NOTES • 3 LESSONS DEVELOPMENT

The lesson's main emphases include

(a) Hoping that their recorded and obvious improvements and achievements will contribute to their self-confidence and inspire a positive attitude to participation in physical activity.

(b) Helping to make them aware of 'How far?', 'How high?' and 'How fast?' in their performances.

Equipment needed

- 15 bean bags
- 15 canes
- 9 tennis balls
- stopwatch
- 5 canes on 10 cones to make hurdles
- marker cones for warm-up and relays

Warm-up activities

(1) The increased forward reach of the foot is quite dramatic when you lift your knee and hip and feel yourself intentionally reaching forward, each stride.

(2) Emphasise 'If you run at the same speed, but add several centimetres to each stride, you must be going faster.'

Timed lap

(1) Of all the activities met in their physical education lessons, running a 250-metre or more lap is one of the most challenging as a measure of endurance and sensible running.

(2) As always, they are told to run on the left side of the track, and to subtract starting from finishing time.

Class activity

(1) Without a bean bag they all practise the start position, side-on to line of put with feet wide apart. Rear elbow is high behind line of put with hand against neck. Forward arm is bent high as balance.
(2) The 'step, close, step' chasse action aims to transfer the body weight forward to assist put.
(3) The final propulsion comes from the rear leg drive, the upper body rotation and the arm thrusting forward from the neck. At the last moment the cocked wrist snaps to send the bean bag off.

Group activities

(1) In the continuing putting practice, we concentrate on technique, by doing the skill slowly enough to feel the several parts. As they travel forward, they must retain the backward lean over the bent rear leg, then rear leg drive; body turn; arm push.
(2) They have three turns at each activity. In the standing high jump, the emphasis is on a dynamic knees bend and legs lift, with feet together. In the scissors jump, they emphasise the 3-count, springy approach and the heel, ball, toes rocking up action.
(3) In the timed sprint remind them of their warming up practice to encourage a good knee lift to increase the stride length.
(4) Co-ordinating the spring from the left foot into a turn on to the right foot, into the wide, side-on position with left foot well forward, needs lots of careful practice in the tennis-ball throw.
(5) Lead leg clears hurdle from the front. Other, trailing leg, has to lift and bend to one side to take it over hurdle before it pulls around and down in front and returns to line of straight running.

Round track relays

Because team running on left of track runs the shortest distance, it is important to reverse the lane positions for the second race. Teams one to five become teams five to one. Teacher calls out results and times both races.

Year 6 • July • Field Lesson 5

LESSON PLAN • 30–50 MINUTES

WARM-UP ACTIVITIES　　　　　　　　　　　3–4 minutes

(1) Walk, side by side, with a partner. When I call 'Go!' one of you show your partner the easy, gentle, relaxed rhythm that you plan to use for the 300-metre run. After 15 seconds I will call out 'Walk!' and the other partner shows his or her 300-metre speed.
(3) Freely, change between walking and short bursts of lap speed running, trying to feel the right, sensible rhythm for you.

TIMED LAP OF 300 METRES　　　　　　　　　4–6 minutes

(1) Relax your hands, arms and legs, and feel a nice, easy rhythm as you run a distance which is a good test of your fitness.
(2) I will call out '50 and 51 and 52 and 53' for example, where the 'and' is 0.5 seconds, to give you a more accurate time. Group one, zero seconds, go! (etc.)

CLASS ACTIVITY; Throwing tennis ball　　　5–7 minutes

(1) Partners, stand apart at distances marked by cones (about 30 metres). Concentrate on jump into your side-on, 2-step throw. Spring and turn to side-on with throwing arm back; then a small cross-over step; then wide stride to throwing position. Arm starts well back, then bends to come over your shoulder, stretching into throw.
(2) Throw for accuracy as well as medium distance. Can you catch your partner's throw?

GROUP ACTIVITIES; Five groups of six　　　15–28 minutes

(1) Measured tennis-ball throw, using standing throw or the spring into a 2-step throw, depending on preference. Judging partner marks where best of three throws lands.
(2) Team standing long jump. Each in turn does a standing long jump from the spot where previous jumper landed. Team distance is marked as challenge to other teams. Technique is to start with feet slightly apart, bend knees and swing arms behind, drive forward with legs and swing arms forward, bend knees to reach as far forward as possible. Next jumper stands in line with toes of previous jumper who stands still on landing.
(3) Choice of timed 50-, 60- or 75-metre sprint. Timekeepers are always at same line. Runners start at one of three marked lines. Team members take turns at being starter/timekeeper.
(4) Scissors high jump over elastic 'bar' tied between high jump stands at about 60 cm. They approach with a slow, springy, 3- or 5-step run-up. Take off is a rocking action along heel, ball, toes of jumping foot. Leading leg swings up strongly.
(5) Relay change-overs within a marked, 20-metre box, with partner. Starter has 10-metre run in, by which time receiving partner has started running. Both plan to make baton change at about 10–12 metres by which time both are running at speed. Partners race other couples.

ROUND THE TRACK RELAY　　　　　　　　　3–5 minutes

Receive the baton, running. Take it with your right hand, then swap it to your left hand for change-over. Receiver, make a good, inverted V with thumb in, fingers out, to receive baton.
After first race, stay at spot where you made hand-over. That will be your starting position for the second race.

The lesson's main emphases include

(a) The teacher's expressed reflection to the class on the way that they have contributed to the success and enjoyment of the lessons by their consistently enthusiastic co-operation.

(b) The pupils expressed reflection on what they think they have achieved together. 'Increased fitness and skilfulness; improved results in running, jumping and throwing; and good fun'.

Equipment needed

- 15 tennis balls
- 5 batons
- stopwatch
- marker cones for throws and relays
- high jump stands and elastic 'bar'

Warm-up activities

(1) It is hoped that partners will advise and guide each other as they try to plan their sensible speed.

(2) The teacher will call for more or less speed as he or she watches them alternating their lap practice with walking.

Timed lap

(1) For this last timed lap in primary school, the quicker runners can be bunched to go off first on the clear track.

(2) During the three lessons repetition of this final lesson, we want them to experience an improved lap time which pleases them, and a quick recovery testifying to improved fitness.

Class activity

(1) The correct technique of transferring weight into a running throw helps their cricket and rounders fielding. The weight transfer applies also to the follow through of the throwing arm after it bends to come high over the shoulder.

(2) As in rounders and cricket a long throw needs to be accurate.

Group activities

(1) Some will now be throwing enormous distances and partners need to have a measurement aid which, ideally, is a tape running parallel with the throws. Lines across the field, 5 or 10 metres apart, will give an instant guide to the 'best of three'.

(2) On way back to start line for a second practice, they can practise an easy hop, step and jump, trying to spread their effort over the three parts, making them almost equal in length.

(3) They can test themselves again at distances sprinted this year, or check how they now perform at a distance sprinted in previous years.

(4) Take-off and landing on grass means that a much scaled-down, safe and easy version must be practised to prevent slipping back at take-off or landing, and falling on a wrist. Run up must be slow, bouncy and well-controlled, not fast and out of control.

(5) Let them see how far they run while calling out 'Running, running, reaching, taking' before offering the right hand back to take the baton. It should be about 10 metres which is a good distance for getting into speed.

Round the track relay

Planning, which is an important feature of physical education in the National Curriculum, is best applied in athletic activities in the relay baton change-over. Both runners should be planning to make the change after at least 10 metres, when the outgoing runner is moving at speed. In the second race, reverse the lane order to give the outsiders the easier inside position.

Year 6 • Team Competition Lesson on Field

LESSON PLAN • 30–50 MINUTES

WARM-UP ACTIVITIES · 3–4 minutes

(1) In your team of six, walk at a brisk pace behind a leader. End person has to jog up to front to become the new leader. When the new leader is in position, the next end person jogs up the front. Twice through, go!

(2) All change to jogging now behind the leader. End runner now has to sprint to front to become next leader. Each end jogger should wait until new leader is in position. Twice through, go!

TIMED PART LAP OF 250 METRES · 4–5 minutes

Plan to run or jog at a steady rhythm that you can keep up all the way. Do not go flying off at such a speed that you have to finish walking and adding lots of seconds to your team score. Subtract your starting time from your finishing time.

GROUP ACTIVITIES; Five teams of six · 20–35 minutes

(1) Timed 75-metre sprint. Each team member is timed individually by another team member. They do one run only after a good, steady crouched start, and they finish fast, running past the line.

(2) Throwing the hoop. Partner marks best of three throws and checks distance on tape at side of area. Throw counts only if it lands inside the permitted, narrow sector, to discourage wild throwing.

(3) Team standing long jump from a line. 1 jumps, lands and stands still so that 2 can line up with his or her toes as take-off place for next jump (etc.). Team result is marked for others to see, and is measured with a tape.

(4) Large-ball throw with each having the best of three marked by a partner. Tape can be laid on grass between this and hoop throw. Emphasise the flat throw so that hoop does not roll on landing. Throw is two handed, from above and behind head.

(5) Hurdling over five hurdles with three steps in between. Each has a 5 points start. If they clear first hurdle correctly, do the three running strides in between, and do not knock any canes off cones, they keep all 5 points. Points are taken off for wrong take-off at first hurdle, for each wrong footwork in between hurdles, and for any canes hit. Teacher advises on scoring.

TEAM SHUTTLE RELAYS; 30 metres · 3–6 minutes

X5 X3 X1 | | X2 X4 X6

1 races to give baton to 2. 1 stays at back of line while 2 races to give baton to 3 and stays at back of line. Each has a 'there and back' run to finish in starting places. Race ends with 5 giving baton back to 1. Baton is carried and received in right hand. Teacher calls out results, first to fifth, and times winning team.

Team Number _____

First place in activity gains five points for a team. Fifth place gains one point.

Event	Individual Results						Combined Result	Place 1st–5th	Points 5–1
	1	2	3	4	5	6			
250 m									
75 m									
Team long jump									
Large ball throw									
Hurdles									
Shuttle relay									
								Total Points Position in Class	

JUNIOR SCHOOL SPORTS DAY FOR ALL

Whole school participation

Vertically grouped teams of eight, ten or twelve pupils with older ones helping and encouraging younger ones. No-one feels left out. The emphasis is on optimum participation, fun and co-operation in activities that all can perform easily.

Competition

Against many other teams, one against one, during the sports, and against all others for final points.

Simple activities for lots of fun and excitement

Relays around marker cone and back to touch next team member
(a) Running, pass baton.
(b) Obstacle, over and under canes on cones at different heights.
(c) Fill and empty hoops with bean bags. First runner takes three bean bags and puts one in each hoop, runs back to touch next runner who brings bean bags back.
(d) Skipping. Pass on rope to next in team.
(e) Bowl a hoop, there and back, pass it on.

Shuttle relays – Half-teams, 15–20 metres apart.
(a) Bean bag on small bat, easy 'egg and spoon'. Run to opposite half of team without dropping 'egg' and pass it on.
(b) Sack race. Pass on sack to one at front of opposite half.
(c) Skipping to other half, pass on rope.
(d) Football dribble around three skittles, pass ball on to next one.

(e) Rugby ball touch down. First runner picks up ball from first hoop; runs to put it in second hoop, touches team mate who returns ball from second hoop to first hoop.
(f) Three-legged race. Couples join left and right hands behind back. Race to change places with opposite front couple.

Team long jump – Each member of team does three consecutive jumps, from a standing position. Next team member jumps from where the previous one landed. Both team distances are marked and compared.

Target aiming –
(a) Quoits to land on cone or in hoop.
(b) Bean bags to land in a container.

Long rope team skipping – to see which team can build up to the greater number, all skipping at the same time.

Netball shooting – to see which team can score more goals, sharing the six balls provided.

Novelty event – Construction activity to build up the higher team tower with the large, wooden bricks in each team's container.

After a first year's successful 'Sports day for all', planning for the following year's event should include providing opportunities for the school's most talented senior athletes to compete against one another in one sprint and one longer distance race while everyone sits down to watch them (and cheer favourites from their team) for the few minutes involved.

TEAM SCORECARD

GLENEAGLES JUNIOR SCHOOL

TEAM NUMBER 4

Activity No.	Activity	Activity Score	Running Score
1	Skipping relay	10	10
2	Three-legged race	5	15
3	Construction activity	10	25
4	Running relay	10	35
5	Team skipping long rope	5	40
6	Bean bag on bat relay	10	50
7	Rugby-ball touch down	5	55
8	Team long jump	10	65
9	Sack race relay	5	70
10	Quoit aiming	5	75
Team Total Score			75 points
Team Position Overall			5th

ORGANISING A SPORTS DAY FOR ALL

(1) Decide how many adults are available. Each activity needs one adult who receives the two teams, explains the activity, judges the result and records each team's score and running score on the score card.

(2) Divide the number of pupils by the number of adults to work out the number of activities. For example: 240 pupils and 12 adults mean 20 vertically grouped teams working their way around 10 activities.

(3) Decide on the activities and vary the nature of consecutive activities for greater interest and variety (as on example score card).

(4) A chart of playground, playground and field, or field with the name of each activity should be copied and put in each classroom and the staffroom.

(5) Adults who are in charge of each event have the rules explained well before the day. A choice of 'Favourite activity to judge' will be appreciated. Judges need a pen or pencil with which to record the team scores.

(6) Choose and number each vertically grouped team. Tell each odd number team where they will start before moving on, clockwise. Tell each even number team where they will start before moving on, anti-clockwise.

(7) Divide the number of minutes available for the whole event by the number of activities, plus two to allow for a 'Getting ready to start'

and a 'Gathering at end to hear results' time. For example, 90 minutes ÷ 12 (10 activities + 2) = 7 minutes 30 seconds per activity.

(8) Emphasise to everyone that only 5 minutes (as in example above) will be allowed for competing in each activity; 30 seconds to record both teams' scores; and 2 minutes to move on to the next activity and have it explained.

(9) The overall organiser starts the Sports Day by ringing a hand bell. After 5 minutes the activity is stopped by the bell. A whistle is blown by the organiser after the half minute during which the two cards are marked, as a signal to move on to the next activity. The hand bell signals the start of the next period of 5 minutes of competition.

(10) At the very end of the activities, when cards are marked, the teachers and their final two teams come to the central meeting area with their apparatus and their completed score cards.

(11) Final scores are recorded on a large score sheet for all to see. In reverse order, each team's score is read out for all to hear. Teams placed sixth to first deserve a special mention, perhaps being asked to stand for a round of applause.

(12) Deserving praise, also, are the organiser, teachers and any parent helpers.

USEFUL ADDRESSES

Amateur Athletic Association of England
225a Bristol Road
Edgbaston
Birmingham
B5 7UB
Tel: 0121 440 5000
Fax: 0121 440 0555
Web address: http://www.british-athletics.co.uk/

Regional Associations of the AAA of England

Midland Counties Athletic Association
Edgbaston House
3 Duchess Place
Hagley Road
Birmingham
B16 8NM
Tel: 0121 452 1500
Fax: 0121 455 9792

North of England Athletic Association
Suite 106
Emco House
5/7 New York Road
Leeds LS2 7PJ
Tel: 0113 246 1835
Fax: 0113 234 3464

South of England Athletic Association
Suite 36, City of London Fruit Exchange
Brushfield Street
London E1 6EU
Tel: 0171 247 2963
Fax: 0171 247 2439

Athletics Association of Wales Office
Morfa Stadium Landmore
Swansea
West Glamorgan
SA1 7DF
Tel: 01792 456237
Fax: 01792 474916

Northern Ireland Amateur Athletic Federation
Athletics House
Old Coach Road
Belfast
BT9 5PR
Tel: 01232 602707
Fax: 01232 309939

Scottish Athletics Federation
Caledonia House
Redheughs Rigg
South Gyle
Edinburgh
EH12 9DQ
Tel: 0131 317 7320
Fax: 0131 317 7321

UK Athletics
UK Athletics
Athletics House
10 Harborne Road
Edgbaston
Birmingham
B15 3AA
Tel : 0121 456 5098
Fax : 0121 456 8752
Web address: http://www.ukathletics.org
Information on courses for primary school teachers: http://www.ukathletics.org/development/educat/teacher.html

Athletics Ireland
11 Prospect Road
Glasnevin
Dublin 9
Ireland
Tel: + 353 1 830 8925 or (01) 830 8925
Fax: + 353 1 830 8763 or (01) 830 8763
Enquires: Admin@AthleticsIreland.ie

INDEX

Other useful teaching resources available from A & C Black

Know the Game series including:

Field Athletics (Second edition)
0-7136-5390-6
Track Athletics (Second edition)
0-7136-5391-4
Hockey (Second edition)
0-7136-4863-5
Netball (Third edition)
0-7136-5266-7
Rugby Union (Fourth edition)
0-7136-5823-1
Rounders (Second edition)
0-7136-5735-9
Cricket (Third edition)
0-7136-5817-7
Tennis (Third edition)
0-7136-5826-6
Baseball and Softball
0-7136-5378-7

General titles:

101 Youth Soccer Drills Vol 1: Age 7–11
Malcolm Cook
ISBN: 0-7136-5153-9

101 Youth Soccer Drills Vol 2: Age 12–16
Malcolm Cook
ISBN: 0-7136-5154-7

Becoming an ASA Assistant Teacher: A Guide
Phil Butler
ISBN: 0-7136-5349-3

Swimming Games and Activities: for individuals, partners and groups of children (Second edition)
Jim Noble and Alan Cregeen
ISBN: 0-7136-5204-7

Available through bookshops. In case of difficulty, contact:
A & C Black, PO Box 19, Huntingdon, Cambridgeshire PE19 8SF
Tel: 01480 212666; Fax: 01480 405014